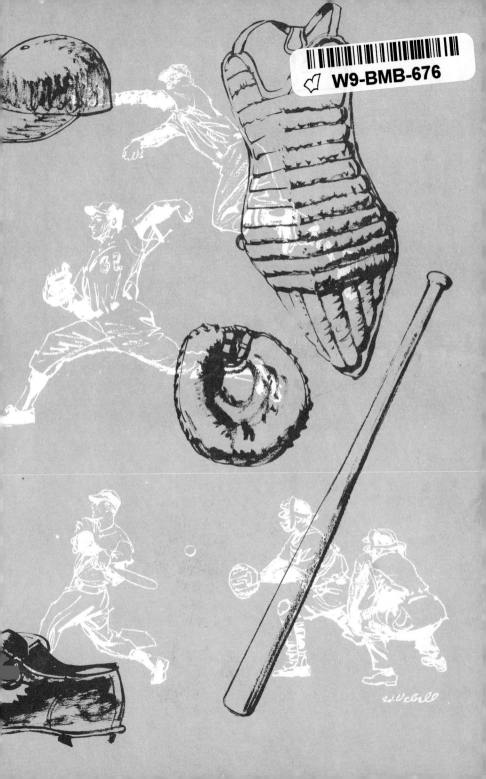

W9-BMB-676

Secrets of Big League Play

This book will help you play better baseball by showing you how the game is played by experienced pitchers, batters, catchers, and fielders in the big leagues. You will find hundreds of examples of how famous big leaguers play each position, as well as hints on how to practice effectively, how to anticipate what the opposing team is going to do, when to back up a member of your team, how to communicate with your teammates, and how to gain confidence. Here are professional secrets that will help you improve your game and become a valuable member of your team.

Secrets of

RANDOM HOUSE   NEW YORK

Big League Play

by ROBERT SMITH

illustrated with drawings
by Ed Vebell

and with photographs

Library of Congress catalog card number: 65-10491

Photograph credits: Brown Brothers, page 98; Culver Pictures, page 9; United Press International, pages 15, 43, 85, 125; Wide World, pages 18, 44-45, 52, 62, 76-77, 78-79, 101, 109, 116, 134-35, 137, 146-47, 148, 165.

CONTENTS

Little League Baseball is greatly pleased to join with Random House in the establishment of a Little League Library. It is our confident belief that the books thus provided will prove both entertaining and helpful for boys of Little League age and indeed for their parents and all who are Little Leaguers at heart.

This is one of a series of official Little League Library Books. Each has been read and approved at Little League Headquarters. We hope they will bring enjoyment and constructive values to all who may have the opportunity of reading them.

P J McGovern

President and Chairman of the Board
Little League Baseball, Incorporated

Secrets of Big League Play

Pitching

1

Pitching, some major league managers say, is 75% of baseball. Some say it is 90%. Whichever figure is right, there is no doubt that the pitcher is the most important man on the field. His skill and his stamina can make the difference between winning and losing a ball game. He is in every play and he is the man in charge when he has the ball in his hand. His arm must be supple, his legs strong, and his mind alert. He must be well rested and in good physical condition. And he must have some reserve strength to draw on when the going gets rough.

Wilbert Robinson, the famous old-time leader of

the Dodgers, had a prejudice in favor of big pitchers. There have been other managers who share this preference. But a player's size is not important as long as he has a sturdy constitution and will work hard to develop strength in his hands, wrists, and shoulders. Scouts will not pass up a slender pitcher if he is wiry. But most scouts will look carefully at a boy's shoulders. A young man is bound to have unusually strong shoulders if he practices throwing as constantly as a pitcher should.

The other basic qualification a scout looks for is control. Control is essential to good pitching and can be achieved only by throwing continually at a target. As a matter of fact, there is one secret that all great pitchers share: *Even in practice, never throw a ball unless you throw it at a target.* The target may be a mark on the catcher's clothing, or a knot on the wall of a barn or fence. A pitcher should practice throwing at a definite target every time he throws the ball.

Before you start to practice, mark off the proper distance from the mound to the plate. (Major league distance is $60\frac{1}{2}$ feet; Little League distance is 44 feet.) As soon as your arm muscles are properly warmed up (it is better to warm up too much than not enough), stand on the spot chosen as the mound and throw full strength and with full arm at your target.

Any mark or spot on the fence or wall will serve as a
good target for practice.

1   2

When Herb Pennock, a Hall of Fame pitcher, was coaching young pitchers and wanted to help them get the full arm into the pitch he used to suggest this: Pretend that there is a table behind you about an arm's length away and that the baseball is lying on the edge of it. Then, looking straight at the target, reach back, pretend to pick the ball off the table, and fire it to the plate. To keep your balance, lift your forward leg. Then grip the ball tightly, keep your wrist limber, and throw the ball hard.

In spring practice big leaguers do not fret if their pitches, thrown full strength, miss the target by a wide margin. It is better to throw the ball with full

3   4

strength and miss the target than it is to steer the
ball with a bent arm and a half push. Throw full
arm and hard until you find where you must release
the ball in order to make it strike close to the target. Don't worry about misses, even if the ball sails
right over the fence. Just keep throwing hard until
you start to zero in. You may not do this the first
day. But keep trying until you can hit close to the
target.

Most big league pitchers use some variation of
the same methods:

1. A forward dip of the body with the arms swung
loosely back.

2. A swing of the arms to bring the arms together in front of the body, then back up over the head, and down behind it.

3. The re-e-e-ach (to pick the ball off the imaginary table), lifting the forward leg off the ground for balance.

4. A strong step forward and a full-arm pitch.

Your weight should be on the ball of the forward foot when you take this step.

The length of the step forward has a lot to do with the accuracy of the throw. A big league pitcher often has to shorten his stride a little in order to get better control of the ball. Practice your own variation of this method until you develop a pitching motion that feels natural to you.

One of the first things a big league coach teaches his rookie pitcher is how to hide the ball. Pitchers discovered long ago that if the batter can see the ball before it is thrown, he can time its arrival. Therefore, pitchers try to hide the ball until the last possible moment. Sometimes a batter or a coach will get a line on the coming pitch if he can see how the pitcher is holding the ball. Therefore, as you face the target, get in the habit of holding the ball either behind your leg or with the pitching hand close to your leg and the back of your hand toward the catcher.

The ball should be held with two fingers on top

Bob Feller of the Cleveland Indians after one of his
"fire-ball" pitches.

of the ball and the thumb beneath it; the fingers should be in contact with the seams. A few pitchers hold the ball *across* the seams for a fast ball and *along* the seams for a curve. But it is best to hold the ball in the same manner for a fast ball and for a curve ball in order to avoid tipping off a sharp-eyed coach.

You should also try to hold your arms the same way for every pitch. If you don't, a batter or a coach may discover what kind of pitch you are planning to use before you even release the ball. When Art Mahaffey, Jr., came up to the big leagues, he learned that coaches on rival clubs were "reading" his pitches because he had gotten into the habit of holding his elbows tight against his chest before throwing the curve and away from his ribs before throwing the fast ball. It is important to avoid habits of this sort.

A pitcher who can put his fast ball exactly where he wants it will be a good pitcher. Yet many young pitchers are impatient to learn trick pitches and curves. Eventually, you will need to know how to pitch a curve. But you must have good control of your fast ball first. When you feel sure that you have this control, you can start practicing the curve.

A ball curves when it moves out of a straight line, either down or sideways. In order to make the ball curve, the pitcher grips it firmly and applies pressure with his thumb and middle (second) finger. He rolls his hand as he throws, and the ball rolls out of the fork between his thumb and forefinger. The forefinger exerts little or no pressure on the ball.

When you first start working on the curve, try to throw the ball with little or no speed on it. In fact, it might be better for you and your teammate to practice without gloves. Skill in pitching a good curve cannot be accomplished quickly because of the danger of hurting or straining your arm. The secret is to toss the ball only a short distance at the start. Try to get as much wrist action and roll in the pitch as possible so that the ball will spin quite rapidly. The spin of the ball is the important factor in determining how good your curve ball will be. As the spin gets better through practice, the distance can be lengthened a little until you are actually throwing the required distance between home plate and the pitcher's mound. At the same time, the ball can gradually be thrown harder.

If you throw a curve ball sidearm, you must be able to throw a fast ball that way too so that the batter can't tell which pitch you are going to use. Walter Johnson, called the fastest pitcher who ever lived, threw sidearm. But most young pitchers find it easier to throw the ball from far back and over the shoulder. Only boys with natural sidearm motion should throw sidearm in the beginning. Overhand pitchers can learn sidearm delivery later to achieve a variety of pitches.

You should practice pitching a curve just as you practiced the fast ball—throwing it at a target over and over again until you can hit the spot you are aiming at. The curve will probably require even more practice than the fast ball, but the results will be worth the effort. With good control and two types of pitches, you are on your way to becoming a valuable pitcher. Other types of pitches can be added after you have acquired confidence and strength. But to start, a curve gives a young pitcher enough variety to keep most young batters off balance.

In throwing the curve, the grip on the ball or the position of the ball in your hand will determine the speed. If the ball is pushed way back in the palm

of the hand, it will slow the pitch down to what is called a change of pace on the curve ball.

Keeping the batter off balance is the true secret of success in pitching. The ability to do this has often made it possible for an older man who has lost his original speed to hold on to a big league job. Satchel Paige, who entered big league baseball when he was 41 years old, after a full career of pitching in the Negro leagues, is a good example. Old Satch would vary his timing on every pitch, sometimes releasing the ball before he finished his stride, sometimes afterward; sometimes shortening his windup, sometimes lengthening it.

An experienced pitcher knows that when a batter begins to meet his pitches solidly, he has begun to time the pitcher's delivery. A batter can do this almost automatically by getting used to the pitcher's rhythm—the time that elapses between the beginning of the windup and the arrival of the ball at the plate. Once when Joey Jay had been hit hard in successive games by the Los Angeles Dodgers, he changed his timing with immediate success. All he did was to shorten the arc of his windup. Instead of a deep dip in front and a generous sweep of his arms over his head and behind his neck, he cut down on the whole movement, letting go of the ball a half second or so earlier than had been his habit. As a result, the Dodger batters who thought they were familiar with his rhythm found themselves stepping into the ball just a moment too late and getting very few safe hits off him.

In trying to alter your rhythm, do not change the basic pattern of your pitch. Just make minor adjustments so that the batter is not able to anticipate the timing of your delivery. But varying your rhythm is only effective *after* you have achieved control, and you can do this only through constant practice. Even when you are just playing catch, remember to throw the ball to a target—to the other fellow's belt buckle, his shoulder, or his knee. And each time you throw the ball, reach way back (Dizzy Dean used to call it "rarin' back") to get the full length of your arm into the pitch.

At the beginning, you should stick to a curve

Dizzy Dean in action in spring training, using his famous
"rarin' back" motion.

ball as a means of variety. But after you have gotten good control of your fast ball and your curve
ball, you may want to add change-of-pace pitches
to your repertoire. The secret of all these changes
is to hold the ball so that the fingers do not press
hard enough on it to give the ball its natural spin.
A change-of-pace pitch will be most effective if you
throw it with the same motion you use for your
fast ball.

A change of pace on a fast ball is called a "letup
pitch." This pitch can be accomplished by pushing
the ball back into the palm of your hand, then
going through your motion. As you are about to
release the ball, the thumb grips it tightly and the
first two fingers are stretched out. The ball rolls off
them but does not lose its spin or rotation on the
way to the hitter. This style of delivery is sometimes compared with the motion used when a per-
son reaches out to take hold of a window shade
and pull it down. You will notice that little or no
wrist action is involved in doing this.

The secret to a change of pace on the curve is
its motion, which must be deceptive. Throw the
hitter off guard at the time of actual delivery of
the ball by not gripping it as tightly as you do
when you throw the regular curve. To learn to do
this well takes patience and long hours of practice.

The curve ball which approaches the plate a

split second more slowly than the fast ball will also throw the batter off-stride if he is not expecting it. And he won't expect it if you throw your fast ball and curve ball with the same motion.

Learning to control your basic pitches is most important. But be careful not to put too much stress on control or on pin-pointing the pitches. If you have a good fast ball, it will be alive—that is, it will move naturally out of the straight line. By using this pitch, you can count on nicking the corners of the plate whenever you try to put the ball over. Once in a while, even in the big leagues, a pitcher will become so concerned with putting the ball into a spot about as big as a dime, that he will unconsciously take something off the fast ball and throw it with just a little less strength, making it easy to hit. That is often what is happening when a good pitcher starts to give up home runs: He is trying to pinpoint a pitch and forgets that it is more important to put his full strength into it.

In pitching to a batter, you must think of the target first. Make it a specific, visible target—not just an imaginary spot in the air. Focus your eye on it, and do not look anywhere else as you pitch. Your muscles will adjust automatically to the distance and position of the target, just as they do when you reach to pick up something, or when you place your feet while running downstairs. The tar-

The great pitching motion of Bob Turley.

get should be on the catcher, not on the batter. Pick out his left or right shoulder, his left or right knee, or the edges of his chest protector. If he can give you a good stationary target with his glove, fix your eye on that. During a game, however, he may place his glove in a position that will mislead the batter. Then you should pick a target on the catcher's body.

When the batter stands in his normal batting position, the strike zone is the area between his knees and his shoulders and is the width of the plate. (If he crouches a bit, as Mickey Mantle does, the strike zone shrinks a little.) Think of the strike zone as an imaginary oblong "hole" to pitch through. In your mind, sketch this imaginary hole against the catcher's body and then decide on the spot on his body that you will use as your target. Perhaps the catcher's armpit nearest the batter will mark the upper inside edge of the strike zone. That is often a good target for a fast ball. The lower outside edge of the zone may be marked by the catcher's knee which is away from the batter. This area is frequently the best target for a curve.

The simplest method of placing the pitch is this: high and inside (sometimes called "high and tight"), then low and outside ("low and away"). Of course an experienced pitcher will vary this pattern in many ways. And it is important to pitch to different spots so that the batter can't get a line on the ball.

In amateur competition, many batters will go after the first ball pitched. You should make sure then that your first pitch is in the strike zone, and that you have something on it—get your full strength into it if it is a fast ball, or "pull down" sharply on it if it is a curve. But be sure not to throw so hard that your control suffers. In attempting to throw too hard, you can upset your natural motion and smooth body action.

Most pitchers at the start of their careers have only two basic pitches and only one of these is really good. If your strong point is your fast ball, use it at once to get a jump on the batter. But do not give up on your curve. Use that when you can afford to put it where it will not be hit—only when you are ahead of the batter in the count. By showing the curve to the batter every now and then, you will remind him that you have another pitch that he must be prepared for.

Getting the ball over the plate or into the strike zone does not mean that you must throw it over the *middle* of the plate. You will learn as you practice that a live pitch thrown over the plate will veer out of the straight path enough to cut the corners—the few outer inches of the strike zone.

And it is to these outer inches that most of your pitches should be aimed.

You should make up your mind that you are going to get the batter out with your best pitch. When you have him in a hole (when he must try to hit anything that is near the strike zone), give him the pitch that you know is your strongest.

You are not, of course, trying to strike out every batter. There are eight other men on your team who are also trying to put the batter out. It is more important for you to make the batter hit your best pitch, for that will be the one he is least likely to hit well. The batter, naturally, is trying to make you throw *his* pitch—the one he knows he can hit the hardest.

If you get a batter down to two strikes and no balls, you have a tremendous advantage over him. For then you can afford to put your pitches—at least one or two of them—outside the strike zone, sometimes well outside it, and there is a chance that he will swing at a really bad pitch. Usually, however, you should be working the corners and edges of the strike zone, trying to get the ball where it will be called a strike and yet where the batter will have difficulty in hitting it.

In competition, a pitcher usually has two motions—a full motion when the bases are empty and a stretch motion when there are runners on base.

In the reaching back position, the pitcher has his left side toward the batter.

It is well to practice pitching from both positions so that they will feel natural to you and will not cause you to lose control. The full motion gives the pitcher a little better momentum. It usually consists of bending forward at the waist, swinging the arms above the head and down behind it, then going through the "raring back" motion already described. But some pitchers—Bob Turley, when he was with the Yankees some years ago, and Camilo Pascual, of Minnesota in more recent days—have found that they are more effective when they pitch from a "no-windup" position. In cutting down on body motion—by not stretching their arms high above their heads and rocking forward and backward before delivering the ball—they improve their control without losing their "stuff."

Most pitchers will agree, however, that the full windup has certain advantages. It provides more opportunity (through minor changes in timing) to keep the batter off balance, and it allows the pitcher to get full strength into the pitch. When the windup is used by a right-hander, the right foot is on the rubber at the start and the left foot is a step behind the rubber. The pitcher is facing the plate, with the heel of the right foot on the rubber and the ball of the foot extending in front of the rubber. As the windup develops, the right foot is shifted until it is parallel with the rubber. As the pitch is completed, the left foot strides sharply forward and the pitcher gives a good strong shove against the front of the rubber with his right foot. In the middle of the windup, in the reaching back position, the right foot is usually in contact with the rubber and the pitcher actually has his left side toward the batter.

In the stretch position, the pitcher starts out with the rear foot parallel with, and in front of, the rubber. The arms are held loosely above the head. The ball is then brought to a full stop in both hands in front of the body while the pitcher checks the

men on base. It is important to remember that you do not need to see the runner's face when you are checking him. You need to see only his *feet* and the base to check his distance from the base and to note which way he is moving. You will observe that left-handers have an advantage as they stretch in facing the base runner directly. Roger Craig, a right-hander and one of the best pick-off men in the National League, keeps good track of the runners without ever turning to look at them. When he stretches, or as he holds the ball in the stop position, he will turn his head just enough to be able to see the runner's feet.

If the pitcher wishes to move the runner closer to the bag, he throws quickly to the first baseman. But once the pitcher is standing on the rubber he cannot feint a throw to first, nor can he step toward first without throwing the ball there. You will sometimes see a big league pitcher toss the ball almost lazily to first. That is because the runner has dodged back almost as soon as the pitcher began his move. Although there is no hope of catching the runner off base, the pitcher must still go through the motions. This move can occasionally be turned to the pitcher's advantage by using a change of pace in the throw to first. The pitcher may throw the ball at medium speed two or three times, then on the next throw, he can really gun the ball over. This maneuver will not often catch an alert base runner. But a slow man who is not planning to steal is sometimes caught this way. He gets used to jogging back to the bag to beat the easy throw and the sudden fast throw catches him off balance.

As you go through your motions on the mound—either the full windup or the stretch—remember to keep the ball well-hidden from the batter. While you are reading the sign, the ball should remain out of sight behind your leg. Then as you bend forward in the "pump," swing your gloved hand out in front of the ball in order to cover it. As you bring your hands above your head, turn the back of your glove toward the batter so that you do not expose the ball in your hand. Then the batter will not see the ball until it suddenly looms up in front of him on the way to the plate.

In dealing with batters you have never seen before, there are general rules to help you, but they cannot always be effective. You still have to judge a batter by what he does at the plate. Generally, a batter who takes a short stride is not likely to be able to handle a low pitch well. And a batter who stands with his feet close together—and whose stride will therefore be somewhat longer—is likely to be weak on a high pitch. Then there are the heavy hitters, the men who like to take a full swing at the ball each time to try to rocket it out of reach.

As you face the target, hold the ball with the pitching hand close to your leg and the back of the hand toward the catcher.

They can sometimes be "hand-cuffed" by a tight, close pitch which does not enable them to get the full length of arm and bat into the swing.

The pitch intended to get the batter out should be placed where he is least likely to connect with it solidly. If you face a hitter who stands in the outside rear corner of the batter's box, just as far away from the plate as he is allowed to go, and who keeps his feet fairly close together, it may be effective first to "pull him up" with a high outside pitch—one that he has to reach for. Then follow with a close one, hoping to set him up for the pitch you want him to try to hit—an outside pitch. But this time, pitch the ball knee-high, where he is likely to hit it on the ground if he hits it at all. Naturally, these general rules are not foolproof. There have been strong sluggers, such as Ted Williams and Stan Musial, who could hit a tight pitch out of the park. You have to get to know the strength and the weakness of the hitters through observation.

Another good point to remember is not to use your change of pace or your "slow" ball on a weak hitter or on a "poke" hitter. A weak hitter may be waiting for exactly that pitch and perhaps can hit no other. A poke hitter is a batter who holds his bat up short (called "choking the bat") and usually moves around a bit in the batter's box. He depends on placing his hits where they cannot be fielded, so he tries to time his poke to send the ball to a carefully selected spot. A slow pitch gives him more time to place the ball accurately.

Instead of easing up on the weak hitters, you should overpower them. They are the batters who will give you strikeouts and pop-ups. If you have an especially good curve, you can depend on that to retire a large majority of them.

Now and then, a heavy hitter can be made to work against himself, especially when pressure is put on him to deliver a much-needed blow. Big powerful men such as Orlando Cepeda and Frank Howard sometimes strike out on a pitch that almost bounces in the dirt—deliberately aimed at their shoetops by a pitcher who guessed that they were ready to swing at anything within reach.

You should not expect to overpower a good hitter unless your skill is far above the ordinary. Even then it is best not to challenge a good hitter by trying to fire a pitch through the middle of the strike zone or into the spot where you know he meets it best. You must work on him as if he were your only job of the afternoon, taking care to "move" the ball (to pitch to all different corners of the strike zone) so that he does not see the same pitch in the same spot twice in succession. The good hitter may be the man who is fooled by your change of pace, especially if you can throw him a fast ball where he is not likely to swing at it, or not likely to hit it well if he does swing.

But a pitcher must do more than merely throw the ball to the plate. He has to field his position. He must work in cooperation with the men around him to keep the bases covered, to cut off throws or to back up throws from the outfield, and especially to take care of bunts. On *every* ground ball hit to the first-base side of the diamond, the pitcher should move quickly toward first base. He may not always be needed. But he must be on his way at once, so that if the first baseman has to field the ground ball, the pitcher can take the throw at first. He should run to a point about two strides on the home-plate side of first base and a stride inside the baseline before circling to touch the inside of the base as he receives the throw. Once the play is completed, the pitcher should circle back into the field immediately to be prepared to throw the ball if there is a possible play at any other base. If the first baseman fumbles the ball, or if the throw is late, the pitcher should be prepared to stop at the base and stretch toward the ball to "shorten the throw" as the first baseman does when catching a throw at first base.

When a bunt is expected, the pitcher and the first baseman should have an understanding about which one will field the ball if it is placed on the first-base side. Experienced players can tell by the sound of the impact of ball meeting bat whether the pitcher has a chance to field the ball or whether it has been bunted too hard for him to make the play. The second baseman will probably be covering first base if the first baseman is charging in for the expected bunt, so the pitcher can be an infielder on this play. Little Al Jackson, of the New York Mets, is often a fifth infielder on bunts or topped ground balls, and he often helped to win games for himself with his glove. A good fielding pitcher, like Jackson, will handle any bunted ball within reach of the mound. When the ball is fielded, if it can be handled cleanly and quickly, the throw should not be hurried. The pitcher should straighten up, look directly at the target, then fire the ball hard. Trying to steer the ball with a limp throw is likely to send it off course. The throw should be strong and natural.

Of course, if the ball is mishandled, or has backspin that makes it hard to reach in time, the throw may have to be hurried. But it is far better to let the runner have the bag than to hurl the ball wildly without sighting the target. Al Jackson, like an infielder, fields the ball in his natural stride and does not lift his head to sight the target until the ball is securely in his hands. Lifting the head to make ready for the throw before you have the ball is the best way to miss the ball completely. "Keep your eye on the ball" is good advice when fielding as well as when batting.

The pitcher will also have to field bunts on the third-base side, and so he must know if the third baseman is going to charge in or if he is going to stay back to keep the bag covered. Bunts that hug the baseline should be allowed to roll, on the chance that they will roll foul unless you have a good chance to make a play advantageous to your team by fielding the ball. Once the ball gets into foul territory, it should be brushed away immediately so that it will not roll fair again. Get your glove on a bunt just as soon as you know it is foul. In that way you will keep it foul and the runner, if there is one, will be unable to advance.

High pop flies are not to be handled by the pitcher. There have been a few pitchers in the big leagues who can catch pop flies. But most good pitchers get right out of the way and let an infielder or the catcher take over unless the ball isn't hit high enough in the air for anyone else to catch except the pitcher. An infielder gets a better look at the ball than the pitcher does, and he has more room to maneuver. Also he is far more experienced at handling such balls.

On throws from the outfield to third base or to home plate, the pitcher must always run over to back up the baseman or catcher. The throw is not always made, but the pitcher should be in the back-up position when there is a chance of such a throw. An overthrow of third or home plate, if not backed up, will mean an extra run. Also, when a throw gets away from the catcher, the pitcher must run in to keep home plate covered. You should practice these moves until they become instinctive. Break for third or home whenever it looks as if a throw will come in to that base; break for home whenever a ball gets away from the catcher with men on base. It is better to be there when you are not needed than not to be there when you are needed.

These are only some of the things a pitcher must learn. Most of his job he will learn through experience, for there is no substitute for practice in any sport. The muscles will not perform just because the mind understands. They must be trained through endless repetition.

A pitcher must walk to the mound not only convinced that his best pitch will get any batter out but also confident of his ability to throw and control the ball. He should take command when he is out there. He must not allow himself to become frozen to his position. Warren Spahn, the greatest left-handed pitcher alive, is a man who takes full charge of a baseball game. He moves off the mound when he needs a breather. He talks to the baseman behind him. He backs off and surveys the whole situation. He oozes confidence, coolness, and command. He also helps to install confidence in his teammates.

A young pitcher will find these tips useful:

1. Develop control by *always* throwing at a target.

2. Do not be afraid to miss the target at the start.

3. Control your fast ball before you attempt a curve.

4. Control your curve in the same way that you learned to control your fast ball, by throwing at a target.

5. Do not attempt to develop extra pitches until you have complete control of your fast ball and your curve.

6. Get your first pitch into the strike zone.

7. Pitch to the edges of the strike zone. Do not pitch over the middle of the plate.

8. Have confidence in your ability to get the batters out.

9. Cooperate and communicate with the men in the field.

Catching

2

The catcher's first duty is to *stop* the ball. He is probably the most important player on the team— even more important in some ways than the pitcher. But he must stop the ball or he is of no use to his team. It takes a rugged boy to become a catcher. He does not need to be the biggest boy on the team, but he should be the one who is a student of the game, is courageous, and is a leader. And no matter how much he knows, he has to train himself to move in front of the ball and keep it from going through.

A big league catcher like Elston Howard is worth

watching. He does not reach out to snag wide pitches with one hand. He does not stoop and scoop up low throws without looking. When a pitch is wide, Howard slides over to get his full body in front of it. When a pitch hits the dirt, he drops to both knees to block the path of the ball. When a pitch goes over the batter's head, he leaps and reaches for it with both hands.

Someone once asked Choo-choo Coleman, catcher for the New York Mets, why he did not ever seem to let a pitch get by, although his teammates almost without exception dropped throws or fly balls frequently. "I *have* to stop the ball!" said Choo-choo. That is the attitude you must have to be a good catcher.

Some big league catching coaches—Bill Dickey, who made Yogi Berra the great catcher he is, and Jim Hegan—will tell you that a catcher has to be one-handed. This does not mean that he doesn't use his bare hand. He holds his bare hand with his fingers half closed and the back of the hand toward the pitcher until the pitch comes in. Then he slides his bare hand over the ball and traps it in the pocket of his glove. Actually, he catches one-handed with two hands. So with his glove as the target, his body as the backstop, and his bare hand as the trap ready to nail the ball as soon as it hits the target, the catcher prepares to receive the pitches thrown to him.

First of all, a young catcher must get used to the tools of his trade. Big leaguers call these "the tools of ignorance," indicating that no one with any sense would accept the tough job of a baseball catcher. He has to use shin guards, a chest protector, a glove, and a mask. The shin guards and chest protector are easy to get used to. But using the glove and the mask requires some skill.

The glove is no longer shoved onto the hand so that it covers the palm—as it was years ago when Bill Dickey was catching for the New York Yan-

kees. Now it is used as a trap that is manipulated by the fingers. The hand goes only part way into the glove. Yogi Berra and some other catchers have always kept one finger outside the glove to protect it from pounding. The fast pitches are really caught on the fingers now, and by changing off the first two fingers you can ease the punishment a little. The trick of using the glove this way is not difficult to learn but it does take practice.

It may take more time to become accustomed to the mask. First, you have to learn through experience that foul balls will *not* go through the bars of the mask; they will just bounce off harmlessly. Once you are confident of that, you can crouch behind the plate and await any pitch without blinking. But you must learn to get your mask off as soon as the ball has been hit. Shove your mask up and off in your bare hand and toss it in the opposite direction after you have determined the direction in which the ball has been hit. This is worth practicing again and again. Getting the mask off widens the angle of your vision so that you can spot a high pop foul more quickly, follow a bunt more easily, or get the range of a throw as it is coming in from the outfield. When you shove your mask off, you must get in the habit of flinging it *away* from the ball. A World Series was once lost because a Boston catcher dropped his mask be-

Yogi Berra, when he was catcher for the Yankees, waiting for a pitch. The batter is Harmon Killebrew of Minnesota.

Dodger's catcher, Roy Campanella, has ripped off his mask and is ready to grab the ball. Hank Bauer of the Yankees, attempting to bunt, popped the ball up behind the plate.

tween his own feet and a descending foul. He tripped
over the mask just as the ball came down.

It requires hours and hours of practice to master
the techniques of catching. Only then can the
catcher concentrate on his job of calling the pitches
and guiding the team. Because he has the whole
team in his view and all the players can see him,
the catcher is usually given the job of directing
traffic in the infield. But his most important job is
signaling for the pitches and catching them when
they are thrown. He gives his signals while squatting comfortably on his haunches. Elston Howard
keeps his feet several inches apart and squats down
easily to signal, with his fingers held high up against
the inside of his thigh.

Howard and his pitcher always talk over their
complete strategy beforehand so that there will be
no major disagreements during the game. The
catcher should know what the pitcher's best pitch
is and should call for it to try to get the batter
out. Occasionally during a game, pitcher and catcher
meet part way to the mound to discuss just how to
pitch to a batter who is coming to the plate. If
there is a man on base, Howard will turn to the
umpire and ask him to call time. (Only the umpire
can call time. But he always does so when a
player requests it.)

From pitch to pitch, the catcher signals what he

wants the pitcher to throw. The pitcher may "shake him off" with a flick of his glove. Or he may use some secret signal to tell the catcher what he wants to throw. But both pitcher and catcher should always know what is coming. The signals are simple. In fact, when there is no one on base, and no one in a position to see the catcher from the same angle as the pitcher does, almost all teams use the same signals for the basic pitches: one finger for the fast ball and two for the curve. Ballplayers sometimes refer to these pitches as number one and number two. (Some ballplayers like to call the curve ball "Uncle Charley.") A closed fist usually calls for the change up, whatever it may be.

The signals must be concealed from the rival coaches and from the batter. Keeping the fingers tight against the inside of the thigh conceals them from the coach at first base. To hide them from the batter and from the coach at third, the catcher rests his gloved hand on his left knee (assuming that the catcher is right-handed) so that the glove blocks the view from above and from third base. The pitcher does not need to study the signal. All he needs is a quick look. The signal can be laid against the thigh, with the glove blocking all view. Then the glove can be swung back just long enough for the pitcher to get the message. Unless the pitcher gives some sort of negative sign, it is understood

The catcher signals while squatting comfortably on his haunches.

that the catcher will get the pitch he has called for. He may provide a further signal by holding his glove briefly in his bare hand to indicate, in accordance with some agreed method, *where* the pitch is to be thrown—high, low, tight, or away. Or there may be a second finger signal used for that purpose.

Once the signal has been accepted, the catcher

comes out of his squat into a sort of semicrouch. He stands as close to the plate as he can so that he can grab foul tips quickly and is able to get his throws away rapidly. He holds his glove so that the whole flat face of it is toward the pitcher, thus providing a good big bull's-eye target. He should reach forward with his mitt to meet the ball. This will help him to catch more foul tips and to catch borderline pitches in the strike zone. It is very important for the catcher to have a good mitt with plenty of padding in it and the best available mask, chest protector, and shin guards so that he can do his job without fear of injury. The left foot is moved slightly ahead of the right foot, and the feet are wider apart than they are when he is squatting. The fingers of the bare hand are folded—not closed into a tight fist, but just held together the way you would hold them inside a mitten to warm them on a cold day. Pitches that come in above the waist should be caught with the glove hand held fingers up. Pitches that come in below the waist should be caught with the fingers down. If the pitch is wide, as we have already warned, the catcher must slide over, moving the foot nearest the ball first, so that his legs are never crossed. If the pitch is in the dirt, the catcher must drop to his knees and block it when there is a man on base.

The catcher should use the same stance for re-

ceiving one pitch as he does for another. Once
when Bill Dickey had first come into the big leagues
with the Yankees, he lost a game without realizing
it by standing up and moving close when he called
for the fast ball, and by staying in his crouch after
he had called for a curve. The Philadelphia team
was able to "read" the pitches because of this and
bombed the pitcher.

It is the job of the catcher to know the pitcher—
not only to know his best pitch but also to know
his best pace. Some pitchers do their best when
they work quickly, with little time lost between
pitches. These are usually men who can concentrate on the job and who possess great stamina.
Other men tend to lose control when they hurry.
The catcher can remind such men to slow down
by holding on to the ball a few extra seconds before returning it, by returning the ball to a baseman instead of to the pitcher, or by walking a few
steps out in front of the plate before snapping the
ball back.

Many pitchers when they lose control start to
throw the ball higher and higher. The catcher can
help steady a pitcher who does this by offering a
good low target with the glove and by slowing his
pace by encouraging him to get off the mound,
move around on the grass a bit, breathe deeply,
and look over the whole field.

In most cases an alert catcher can tell whether his pitcher is getting tired by studying his delivery. A tired pitcher seldom makes a complete follow-through after releasing the ball.

It is an important part of a catcher's job to throw, and he must practice continually at getting his throws off fast and hard. Yogi Berra is still horrified when he recalls his first World Series against the Dodgers. He had not yet learned to get his throws off fast, and the Dodger speed boys, led by Jackie Robinson, stole bases almost at will. Eventually, under Bill Dickey's patient teaching, Yogi became expert at getting a fast accurate throw off to second base to nail a runner. Bill Dickey taught him to let his hands, holding the ball, ride right back with every pitch, carrying the ball up beside his right ear, while his weight shifted to his right foot. In this way, he was *always* ready to throw. He made his throw overhand, stepping forward strongly with his left foot and snapping the ball quickly, without windup or extra step. And he always threw the ball on a low line, as if he were trying to hit the bag with it.

Before he developed accuracy, he threw many balls into centerfield. But Dickey taught him to put the full strength of his body into every throw and not to worry about the ball going over the baseman's head. Accuracy is achieved by practice, not

Roy Campanella, tossing off his mask after Phil Rizzuto
of the Yankees pops a foul.

by pushing the ball cautiously at half speed toward the target.

A catcher is a fielder, too, and has important work to do in catching pop-ups and in fielding bunts. Before he starts the day's work, Elston Howard always looks up to judge the position and the brightness of the sun. This is a habit you should try to acquire. Then you will be able to judge whether a foul pop is going to go up into the sun. If it is, you can go after it from an angle that will keep the sun out of your eyes. When the ball appears to go straight up off the bat, get your mask off immediately and toss it away from the ball. At the same time look up quickly to find the ball and start after it. You can always give up on it if you see it is going out of play. But if you wait to see if it is going to be in play, it may be too late to start after it.

Foul pops are among the hardest balls to catch because they invariably have a great deal of spin that makes them tend to hop right out of the glove. So no matter how easy the play looks, take each foul pop seriously and never be careless about gloving it. Hold the glove at eye level and hold it flat. Keep your eye on the ball every moment. Smother the ball quickly with your bare hand and squeeze it tight when it hits the glove. Tell yourself you *must* catch this ball and hold it. It will put the batter out and make your pitcher's day that much easier.

But if you miss the catch, do not kick the dirt or slam your glove. The catcher is supposed to be the steady man on the team and should set a good example for the others. The important thing is to get on with the game.

Bunts that are pushed out in front of the plate belong to the catcher. Scramble after a bunt quickly, without waiting to see who else may be trying for the ball. If you can get to it, it is too far away from any other player. Trail bunts to the left, *always*. In that way, you will be in a position to throw quickly to first. Never try to pick up a moving ball in your bare hand. It will be spinning too hard for you to grip it quickly. Put your glove in front of it, and scoop the ball into the glove with your throwing hand. Then pluck it out and throw it. If the ball stops dead before you get to it, then you can pick it up in your bare hand and throw it. But until the ball is safely in your hands, never take your eye off it. When you have it tight in your throwing hand, straighten up and look right at the target. Then fire it with all your strength to the *in-side* of the bag in order to avoid hitting the runner.

It is the catcher's job not only to throw out base runners who attempt to steal but also to help the pitcher hold runners close to the bag so that

they will not get too long a lead. If a runner is slow in returning to the bag after a pitch and is taking a long lead each time, fire a ball down there immediately after a pitch. You should arrange a signal with your first baseman so he will know when you intend to try to catch a runner this way. But you can sometimes hold the runner close to the bag just by jumping into throwing position and faking a throw.

With a man on third base, you can naturally expect an effort to score—especially if there is one out and a good bunter at the plate. Be careful not to let the runner take too long a lead. If he wanders too far from the bag, you can drive him back with a quick, hard throw. Don't be afraid to throw to the bases. Develop confidence in your own accuracy by continually throwing to a target. Practice snapping into your throwing position from your catching crouch and letting your throw go with all your strength to first, to second, to third. When a runner knows that you are willing and able to throw to any base, he is going to watch you carefully and leap back to the base even when you fake a throw in his direction.

The only catcher who ever won the Most Valuable Player award three times was the Brooklyn Dodgers' Roy Campanella, whose career was cut short by a tragic accident. Campy was always ready to throw, always loose and mobile behind the plate. As he caught every pitch, his right hand would ride back into throwing position so that the ball seemed to be continually cocked right behind his ear, ready to be rifled off in any direction. Runners on third base, especially, learned to be extremely cautious when Campy was working, for he could and would snap a throw down if the runner took an extra step lead.

A catcher, even more than a pitcher, must learn

the habits of the batters, so that he can call the right pitches and can warn the fielders how to position themselves. There are some batters who have a habit of slicing most of their hits—hitting them to the "opposite" field. Such a batter, if he is left-handed, will hit best to left field. If he is right-handed, he will drop hits in right. With such a man at the plate, the catcher must check to be sure the outfielders have not shifted into the wrong spots. Often, by warning the right fielder to stay nearer the foul line, or even to move in several strides closer when one of these "opposite-field" hitters is up, a catcher can help turn a safe hit into an out. Because the catcher can see all the fielders, and because it is his job to study the habits of batters, he is in the best position to offer such suggestions.

In amateur baseball and in school baseball, there are many batters who swing late, especially if the pitcher has good speed. A late-swinger is not a good hitter and he will often hit soft fly balls that fall short in the "opposite" field. If the fielders make the conventional shift (to the right when a left-hander comes to bat, to the left for a right-hander), they may leave room for such a batter to drop in many bloopers. But if the catcher is able to spot and remember these hitters, he can help the pitcher a great deal by placing the fielders so that they can take advantage of the batter's weakness.

Inexperienced batters are often uneasy in the box and fail to get a good toehold. When you spot one of these jittery fellows, you can often get him out by pitching him tight with a fast ball, so that he jumps away from the plate (if your pitcher throws sidearm, he will scare the batter even more), and then feeding him a curve on the outside corner, which will often find him too far away to reach it properly.

A strong arm is so important to a catcher that throwing practice to strengthen the arm and develop accuracy should be a daily routine. Stretch the distance between you and your partner until it is as far as you can throw without taking an extra step or putting a strain on your arm. Then throw to the other fellow's knees, keeping your eye on the target and throwing (after you are warmed up) with your full strength.

A good catcher is usually a "talker" as well as a signal-giver and pitch-receiver. Almost every great catcher from Connie Mack to Yogi Berra has been a talker. In fact Connie Mack, who began to play in the bare-hand dark ages of the game, was long known as "the talking catcher." Sometimes these men talk to distract the batter. But they are also trying to build up the pitcher's confidence, to develop spirit in the team, to keep the infielders on their toes, and to get the whole team to work and move together.

One of the greatest catchers in history, Mickey Cochrane, was well known for his special ability to build up a pitcher's confidence. Even when a pitcher was being bombarded, Mickey would walk part way to the mound to return the ball and reassure the pitcher: "Just lucky hits! These guys can't touch you! Pour the ball in there!"

It is important for a catcher to work well with his pitcher. He should never heckle him or argue with him. And if he can assure the pitcher that he can get the batters out, he is making a real contribution to the game.

The catcher is always the first to notice that a pitcher is weakening and sometimes he can see why. You may find that your pitcher, under pressure, is beginning to miss the strike zone by increasingly larger margins. Try to steady him by offering a solid low target that will bring his pitches down. But perhaps, because of his anxiety, he is beginning to overstride. If you discover this, you should carry the ball back to the mound and tell him about it. At the same time you can slow him down and lessen his anxiety by holding the ball a while and by encouraging him to believe that he can get the batter out. Remind him to pitch to *you*, to take his time, to forget the batter, and get the pitch in there.

If you watch any of the great catchers—Earl Battey, Elston Howard, John Roseboro—you will notice that they always fire the ball back to the pitcher with real zip, unless they actually carry it part way out to him. This is not because they are angry with him or want to wake him up, but because they do not want to give base runners extra time to start. In amateur baseball, where catchers will sometimes flip the ball gently back from behind the plate, a runner on first can often make a lot of distance between the time the catcher lets go of the ball and the time the pitcher has received it and is ready to throw it to second. So try to make it a habit to snap the ball back with good speed. You won't hurt the pitcher. And you will not be giving the runner an advantage. But when there is a man on first, you should always look down there after every pitch. If the man has not returned to the bag, bluff him back by pretending to throw. If he has taken a big lead and has not moved back quickly, rifle the ball to the first baseman to try for the out. Even if you do not get the man out, you will keep him cautious, and he will not stand out on the baseline the next time you have the ball.

Some young catchers find that the hardest job, after the basic skills have been mastered, is to tag a runner who is trying to score. The catcher, if he has the ball in his hand, is permitted to block the baseline in order to put the tag on the runner, and often the runner will pile into the catcher and bowl him over. Because of this, an inexperienced catcher will often try to keep one eye on the runner and one eye on the throw coming to the plate. As a result, he may miss the throw completely or may fail to catch it cleanly enough to hold onto the ball when the runner bumps into him.

It is not necessary to shield the plate with your body in order to tag a runner. Your foot is probably long enough to block off the whole front end of the plate. And all you want to do is to hit the runner with the ball or with the glove holding the ball. If the ball is coming from left field, or from the left-field area, you should stand on the first-base side of the plate to await the throw. As the ball comes close, and you see you are going to be able to catch it in the neighborhood of the plate, you should go to your left knee, with your right foot at right angles across the baseline to shut off the plate. When you have the ball securely in both hands, bring the glove, the ball, and your bare hand down (within the pocket of your glove) in front of your right foot so that the runner, if he slides,

Elston Howard, Yankee catcher, tags Senators' John
Kennedy at the plate.

must slide right into them. If he does not slide, he
will run into you and—if you keep control of the
ball—he will be out.

If the ball comes in front of the right-field area,
you should straddle the plate and use your left foot
to close off the third baseline.

If you see that the throw is not coming to the
plate, you must move to get in front of it. Your
first job is to get hold of the ball. Do not try to

watch the runner. You know where he is headed. Get in front of the ball, stop it, squeeze it, lay it on the runner if you possibly can, diving toward him if you must.

Sometimes, you will get the ball well ahead of the runner and he will retreat to third. Let him see the ball in your bare hand and chase him back. But until the pitcher has had time to get behind you and back you up, do not let go of the ball. You probably will not be able to catch him. But if he commits himself to a fast return to third, fire the ball hard to the third baseman and then get off the baseline. If you block the line without the ball in your hand, the runner will be awarded home plate free if he turns and collides with you. If he turns and starts back, your job is to back up the fielder who is chasing him. This means letting the runner pass you (assuming that the pitcher has come in to cover home) and getting in position to take a throw if the runner starts back toward third.

Amateur catchers have a little trouble in keeping signals hidden from the other team. Therefore, when there is a base runner in a position to see your finger signals to the pitcher, you must find a way to show the signals to the pitcher without the runner seeing them.

The big league method is to agree on a code number. If the code is number five, it means that the signal will be given after five fingers have been shown. The catcher will show two fingers, then one finger, then two fingers again. Then the *next* sign will be the real one. But the catcher will then give a few more so that the runner will not know which one is the actual signal. In the next series, the catcher may show three fingers, then two, then the real sign, then another sign or two. And so on. Although big league observers as crafty as Leo Durocher or Solly Hemus or Brooks Lawrence could figure out a code like that in a short time, it is very unlikely that a young ballplayer is going to have time to decode it and tip off the pitches you are calling. Perhaps if you play several games against the same team you may want to make the system a bit more complicated. You might change the code number on each pitch, in accordance with a sign given by the pitcher—rubbing the knee for one, the belt for two, the chest for three, and so on. But it is best not to engage in complicated maneuvers like this unless there is a good reason to think that the signs are being stolen and that the theft is hurting you.

These are the chief points for a catcher to remember:

1. You *must* stop the ball. Get your body in front of the ball if the pitch is wild.

2. Catch with one hand, keeping your bare hand

folded (not clenched) until the ball is in your glove.

3. Snap your body and arm into throwing position every time you receive a pitch.

4. Show the flat of your glove to the pitcher as a target.

5. Offer a low target if the pitcher is wild.

6. Hide your signals.

7. Watch the ball, not the runner, when the throw is coming home.

8. Talk it up! Encourage the pitcher.

chapter

3

Batting

3

Of all baseball skills batting requires the most constant and unremitting practice. Even a great hitter can lose his batting eye if he skips too many practices or starts to swing lazily at bad pitches. Ted Williams, who probably had a finer batting eye than any ballplayer who ever lived, practiced hitting morning and night. As a boy, he would practice before school or work, and then whenever he had a moment to spare afterwards. When he was in the big leagues, he would practice his swing almost anywhere. Once he accidentally smashed a bedstead in a hotel room while he was practicing his swing in front of a mirror. He never failed to listen to advice from other good hitters, and he would study their stance, their swing, and their grip, looking for ideas to improve his own batting.

So if you intend to be a good hitter, start immediately to study and practice in every spare moment, even when there is no baseball to swing at.

The first thing to do is select a bat that fits you. Many young ballplayers develop bad habits by trying to swing too large a bat. Using the same weight and size bat that Mickey Mantle uses is not going to make you hit the way Mickey does. You must use a bat that is suited to your size and muscular development. Babe Ruth used a bat weighing nearly four pounds; it would seem like a telephone pole to one of today's hitters. Now the bat is whipped around quickly, with sharp wrist action, and it is the speed and timing of the swing, rather than the weight of the club, that provides the distance.

Heavy bats are useful in developing the arms and wrists, and it is often good to practice with a bat that is a few ounces heavier than the one you plan to use. When you select a bat, try to get one that will not droop if you hold it out horizontally, one that you can keep straight without any undue strain on the wrists, and one that you can swing swiftly and smoothly. If you are small-boned and slightly built, do not try to imitate the biggest fellow on the team. Only by experimenting will you learn how heavy and how long a bat to use, and whether to use a "choke" grip. Your decision may depend on the pitcher you face.

Your batting stance, too, should be adjusted to your size and build. It should, above all, feel natural and easy. If you are big and have strong wrists and shoulders, you may want to dig in solidly and go for the long ball with a full swing. Most batters in the major leagues spread their feet about the width of their shoulders and stand far enough back in the batter's box so that they won't stride out of the box with the front foot when they swing. Power hitters know that they can swing a light bat faster than a heavy bat and that the speed of the swing determines the distance the ball is hit. Place hitters who don't have power usually swing heavier bats which are bigger around and provide more of a surface with which to contact the ball. Even power hitters know that they should not swing hard at the ball when the count is two strikes against them. With only one strike left, they concentrate on meeting the ball.

There are almost as many different stances as there are batters. Stan Musial seemed to twist himself right away from the pitcher and hit from a half-crouch. Ted Williams stood up straight, with his feet well spread and took a relatively short stride.

Mickey Mantle bends over a little to shorten his "strike zone." In general, however, it is good to avoid an exaggerated crouch at the plate. Place your front foot wherever you can achieve the best balance. Most major league batters use a closed stance with the front foot closer to home plate than the back foot, and the back foot close to the rear line of the box. Putting a little extra weight on the front foot, without overbalancing, will keep you from taking an exaggerated stride into the ball. Overstriding is what causes so many young batters to hit under the ball, to pop it up, to miss it altogether, and to meet it with only part of their strength.

All batters should try to hit line drives most of the time.

There was an old batting champion, Jesse Burkett, who said that the real secret of batting was "that old *confeedience*"—his way of pronouncing confidence. It is true that unless you stand at the plate with the conviction that you can hit the ball, your chances of success are greatly diminished. A good comfortable stance, one that lets you feel balanced and ready to step in any direction, helps provide confidence. Plenty of batting practice does the rest.

Before you ever stand at the plate, practice gripping and holding the bat correctly. If the bat is

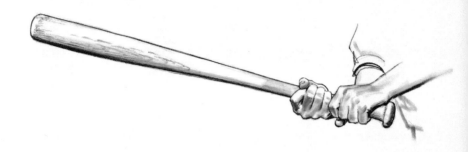

the right weight for you, you can take hold of it just above the knob and swing it without having it droop from a level line. But if you feel more confident when you hold the bat a little shorter, do so. Nellie Fox and Red Schoendienst held the bat well up on the neck, two inches or more from the knob. Your elbows, as you stand facing the pitcher, should be well away from your body, with the elbow nearest the pitcher lifted until it practically points at the pitcher's face. By freeing your elbows from your body, you will have a chance to swing the bat freely and easily and yet still be able to cover the whole strike zone.

The bat should be cocked at an angle between the head and shoulders with the knob about at the rear shoulder. A few batters hold the bat level or even let it droop, and then have to cock it when the pitch comes. But the best way to develop a

smooth swing is to get the bat back in front of your rear shoulder, keeping your front elbow high, and to take a full swing at the ball. Practice your stance, grasp, and swing until they become so natural to you that you can forget about them. Then the important thing is to practice keeping your eye on the ball.

Keeping your eye on the ball is not as simple or

natural as it sounds. There are relatively few young batters who really keep their eyes on the baseball when they stand at the plate. Even in the big leagues there are men who will occasionally take their eyes from the ball to pick out the spot where they want to hit it. But the ball should be on your mind and in your sight from the moment the pitcher gets ready to throw until the ball nears your bat. As a matter of fact, it is excellent practice to stand at the plate with the bat in your hands while the pitcher and catcher throw the ball back and forth. Follow the ball with your eyes from the time the pitcher takes hold of it to the moment it passes you. Do not turn your head to do this. Do that eight or ten times every day before you take any practice swings, until your eyes automatically follow the ball the whole way in.

When you are ready to swing, focus your eyes on the ball. Find it in the pitcher's glove, if you can, and never take your eyes from it. Try to follow the ball to your bat without turning your head. Do this every time you swing until it becomes second nature to you to sight down the bat to see where the ball and bat meet.

In swinging at the pitch, whip the bat forward with your wrists. This will give you the whole length of the bat to hit with. Step toward the pitch and swing right through the ball. Do not try to "kill"

Roger Maris has his eyes focused sharply on the ball as
he starts to swing.

Roger Maris steps into the ball . . .

it. If you start to think about driving it out of the
park, you will begin to overstride, to lunge at the
ball, and to throw your bat out of line. Just meet
the ball smoothly, easily, and quickly. And drive

. . . as he connects for a homer.

your bat all the way around as if it were a big knife slicing the ball in half.

Many good sluggers admit that they began to hit home runs only when they forgot about trying for them. Elston Howard, for instance, hit many home runs when he thought only of getting a hit.

Of course there are experienced players who have developed supreme confidence in their ability to hit any ball pitched. Roger Maris and Willie McCovey will actually "uppercut" the ball to drive it into the seats. But that is something you can think about only after you have been hitting the ball successfully for many seasons. In the beginning, just concentrate on getting hits.

As you stand at the plate, you may want to keep your arms loose by taking practice swings. When you do this, swing just the way you would swing at a pitch—more slowly perhaps and without the strong follow-through—but on the same level. Big league batting coaches often tell young players to aim their hits at the pitcher—to swing the bat as if the pitcher's head was the ball and the bat could reach it. This keeps you swinging on a level with your wrists and gets you in the habit of meeting the ball in front of the plate.

In amateur practice there may be times when the batter has only a backstop behind him, and he will be tempted to reach out with his bat to stop bad pitches. This is a very bad habit. *Never* swing at a bad pitch in practice and never reach out to knock a bad pitch down. In batting practice make the pitcher give you the pitches you want and let *all* the bad ones go through to the backstop. Watch them all the way. But don't try to stop them.

In amateur and school baseball, bunting is far more important than it is even in the major leagues. Among younger ballplayers, bunts can often be safe hits, or at least they can get runners on base. This is because there are so many young players who cannot throw strongly or accurately enough.

Bunting is also excellent practice because the batter is required to eye the ball closely and to catch the ball on the bat. The first type of bunt to practice is the sacrifice bunt, the bunt that the pitcher, when he is up at bat, is so often called upon to execute if there is a runner on base ahead of him. No effort is made to conceal from the opposition the batter's intention to bunt. The batter squares around in the front of the batter's box, facing the pitcher directly, and holding the bat with hands far apart. As the ball comes to him, he tries—with his arms fully extended and the bat held level—to block the path of the pitch. If a bunt is missed in this position, it is usually because the batter stabs at the ball. He should just catch the ball on the bat.

Hold the bat with the front hand (the left hand, for a right-handed batter) nearest the handle, and the rear hand about at the label. The bat should be in fair territory, held at the top of the strike zone, and should cover the width of home plate.

Hold the bat well forward in the fingers so that the fingers will not stop the ball. And hold it loosely. If you grip it too tightly, the ball may rocket back on the fly to the pitcher for an easy out. The bat must give just a little to make the ball drop to the ground.

When the sacrifice bunt is in order, make sure
that the pitch is in the strike zone. Do not go fish-
ing after balls that are impossible to bunt (except
when you *must* protect the runner, as in the sui-
cide squeeze play). And do not stab at balls that
you do not intend to bunt. When the right pitch
comes, catch it on the bat and be sure it isn't
bunted in the air.

Bunting for a base hit is quite a different oper-
ation. When you execute this type of bunt, you
must conceal from the opposition that you intend
to "lay one down." A left-handed batter is better
equipped for this sort of bunt because he need not
run across the pitch. He can merely "drag" the ball
along with him as he starts for first base. Still there
have been some fine right-handed bunters. One of
the best was Phil Rizzuto, former shortstop of the
New York Yankees. Phil was a solid hitter when he
was swinging for long ones so that pitchers treated
him cautiously and basemen did not crowd in on
him. When he planned to bunt, Phil would take his
warm-up cuts at the air while he stood in the box
and would not alter his stance at all as the pitch
came down. As a right-handed batter, at the last
second he would slide his right hand up on the bat,
about as far as the label, and start to move toward
first, with his right foot moving forward as he pivoted
on his left foot. His right foot didn't come down out-

side the batter's box until the ball had met the bat. He would keep his eyes on the ball and catch it on the bat close to his body to send it spinning down the third-base line. But Phil would not wait to see if it rolled fair or foul. He knew he needed every split second to reach first base, so he would tear off at top speed. More often than not, he was nearly on the bag before the ball was fielded.

Mickey Mantle does a fine job of dragging a bunt. Because he has the extra advantage of power, no fielder dares to move close. He, too, starts off on his right foot and slides his hand up on the bat at the same instant. But by the time the ball reaches his bat, he has taken a full step toward first. Batting left-handed when he drag bunts, Mantle strides toward first base with his left foot and slides his left hand up the bat handle as the bat goes forward. He times the bunt so that he is striding toward first as the bat meets the ball, but neither foot is outside the batter's box at the time of contact.

A drag bunt, properly executed, rolls out of the reach of the pitcher and the first baseman. But it is not hit hard enough for the second baseman to field the ball and throw out the bunter.

A squeeze bunt, which endeavors to squeeze a runner in from third, is not as common in the majors as it used to be, although teams with good bunters and base runners will use it frequently.

Phil Rizzuto bunts during practice.

When the major league teams use it, they most often resort to the "safety" squeeze—the play in which the base runner does not start from third until the ball has been bunted and is safely on the ground. But in amateur baseball this play can be unusually valuable. It can even score two runs at a time, if there are runners on second and third, because young pitchers are often careless about holding a runner close to second base. So the runner on second can occasionally take a long enough lead to make it all the way home on a well-executed squeeze.

The batter on the squeeze play, like on the hit-and-run, *must* hit the ball. No matter where the pitch is (unless it is an obvious wild pitch), the batter is committed to get his bat on the ball in order to keep the runner from being caught. A foul bunt will at least give the runner a chance to return to third. So when this play is called for and you are the batter, you have no choice of pitches. You *must* get your bat in front of the very next pitch, even if you have to stretch for it.

The hit-and-run play is really what its name implies. It takes a lot of practice for players to become adept enough at placing their hits and at meeting the ball with the bat on command to execute this play as a pure hit-and-run.

In amateur baseball, it is best for the runner to

take off as on a steal and for the batter to hit the pitch only if he knows he can hit it on the ground in the proper direction. If the pitch is too close to him, or is placed so that he is likely to hit it in the air, the batter should let it go and allow the runner to take his chances on the steal. Sometimes the man at bat can help the runner by swinging at the ball and deliberately missing it, just to make the catcher's job a bit harder.

Even half a century ago, when the famous John McGraw was directing the New York Giants, he became disgusted with his team's inability to execute the hit-and-run. He ordered them to make it a run-and-hit—the batter would swing at the ball only when he knew he could place it properly.

The ball is properly placed in a hit-and-run when it is hit behind the runner. Usually, when a runner starts from first to second with a right-handed batter at bat, the second baseman hurries down to second to take a possible throw. This leaves a wide hole between first and second. It is into this hole that the adept hitter tries to place the ball. He does this, if he is right-handed, by holding back the front shoulder and swinging a little later than he would normally.

A left-handed batter has a natural tendency to hit behind the runner. But when there is a left-hander at bat, the second baseman usually allows the shortstop to cover second base on the steal so that the hole is not where it should be. The batter may then hit *ahead* of the runner. But hitting ahead of the runner is dangerous because it often brings the ball to second base before the runner gets there and provides the opposition with a ready-made double play. Don't do it unless you are *sure* the shortstop is moving out of position.

Often in a ball game it is necessary only to get the ball on the ground to give your team a chance to score. This is often true when first base is open and there is a man in scoring position. Under such circumstances, especially late in the game, Casey Stengel usually orders his batters to "butcher-boy" the ball—that is to chop at it so that it will bounce through the infield. This maneuver is also known as a "Baltimore chop" and is sometimes used to take advantage of an infielder who is charging in to field an anticipated bunt. By suddenly swinging with a shortened bat and beating the ball down to the ground, the batter can occasionally bounce the ball right over the infielder's head for a safe hit.

In order to outwit and overpower the pitcher, the batter must learn to guard the plate. He cannot concede any part of it as an area that he cannot reach. As you practice batting, try to discover in what area you find it most awkward to get the bat on the ball. If you find that pitches on the inside of the plate give you trouble, you may need to "open" your stance a little to move your front foot a bit closer to the baseline. If it is the outside edge of the plate that you cannot cover, step closer to the plate and pull your front foot a bit closer to the plate than your rear foot.

Some rookie batters, in their eagerness to cover every part of the plate, develop a bad habit—one that has always irritated Casey Stengel. They bend down, with their buttocks sticking out, and slap at the pitch. A batter must learn to be in balance throughout the swing, not leaning forward, backward, or sideways. He uses his stride, hip pivot, arms, and wrists to put power into his swing.

It is often a good idea, if you are in your batting stance for any length of time, to relax the muscles by bending the knees slightly. But when you do that, take care that you do not tip too far forward. Watch big league batters and pay special attention to the manner in which they keep their hips in position.

Every batter runs into a slump now and then. Often such slumps are psychological in origin and may result from some unconscious flinching, or from the batter's growing conviction that the pitchers know his shortcomings. Sometimes a slump is caused by a little flaw in the stance and swing. For example, a batter who has driven out several long hits may begin to think of himself as a born slugger and start, unconsciously, to turn his head away from the pitch in order to watch the ball go over the fence. Or he may start to lunge at the ball, impatient to get hold of it and drive it out of the park. The batter is probably the last man to notice these faults and so, as they continue to cause him to miss the ball altogether, or to pop it up in the air, he presses more and more, until the fault becomes exaggerated.

One of the first things to do when your batting suddenly falls off is to have someone who knows baseball watch you at the plate and point out to you what it is that you are doing wrong. An adjustment in timing, or a change in the way you address the pitch or cock your bat beforehand, may be all you need to get back in the groove. But do not make the mistake of trying to alter your batting style completely. Confidence is what you need most. And you cannot have confidence unless you feel natural at the plate.

By convincing yourself that the slump is just a temporary setback, you will recover your confidence. You will be able to tell yourself, as you go to the plate, that you can make the pitcher throw the pitch you want and that you can hit it safely, no matter how hard he tries to get it by you. Constant practice at watching the ball and meeting it smoothly and easily with the bat will help you regain your confidence, too.

There are times, of course, when you cannot get your pitch and when you must still hit the ball if you can. A batter cannot become so consumed with desire to improve his own average that he passes up a chance to drive in runs. When a game is close, when there are runners in scoring position, and when time is growing short, you have to consider hitting whatever the pitcher gives you if it is in the strike zone. In such circumstances, the pitcher will try to avoid giving you anything you can hit well and you may have to settle for a ball that is not quite where you would like to have it. But especially in the lower leagues, a batted ball of any sort may possibly bring in a score. In the major leagues a good hitter may even hit a ball outside the strike zone if he is confident that he can drive in a run which will decide a game.

Bear these things in mind when you go to bat:

1. Be confident. Address the pitches aggressively.

2. Take a comfortable stance that allows you to reach any ball in the strike zone.

3. Keep your eyes on the ball.

4. Be satisfied to meet the ball squarely.

5. Run out every hit! Don't wait to see where the ball went.

Fielding

4

The infielder and outfielder must obey the same basic rule as the batter: *Keep your eye on the ball.* The fielder who takes his eye away from the ball to see if there is anyone ready to take his throw is the one who makes the crucial errors. The only exception to this rule is that an outfielder may turn away from the ball and let it out of his sight before he fields it when the ball goes far into the outfield and is in the air so long that there is plenty of time to line it up.

Great fielders, like Tris Speaker, Dominic DiMaggio, Edd Roush, and Willie Mays have been able to "go back" after hard hit balls because they could judge quickly the probable path of the ball. They could then turn their backs and run to the spot where they expected the ball to fall, keeping it in sight and watching it until it fell into the glove. Tris Speaker actually learned to judge the general direction a ball would travel by the sound it made when the bat struck it.

But the real secret of Speaker's skill was endless practice. Old Cy Young, the most durable pitcher who ever lived, used to help Tris, when both were with Boston, by hitting innumerable fungoes over his head. (A fungo is a ball that the batter hits out of his own hand.) Tris would turn at the crack of the bat and try to catch up with the ball and haul it in before it fell. He must have done this a thousand times before he became the best in the business.

In practice, a fungo batter should not merely knock balls where a fielder can catch them easily. He should hit the kind of ball a fielder has to run for; and he should hit them again and again. Although it is true that most outfielders hold their jobs with their bats, no team wants an outfielder who is going to lose ball games for them by letting fly balls fall safely or by allowing a ground ball to roll through him to the fence.

When a big league outfielder runs after a fly ball,

he *always* runs on his toes. Running on the heels jars the spinal column and throws the eyes slightly out of focus so that it is impossible to judge the path of the ball correctly. Notice how Willie Mays turns on the speed when he goes after a long fly. He runs on his toes, like a sprinter, keeping his eyes on the ball. Mays, like all good outfielders, uses two hands on the ball whenever he can, but he takes the ball in one hand if he needs to stretch or jump for it.

An outfielder should never surrender on a ball. If it is going over the fence, the time to give up on it is when you are at the fence and cannot reach it with your best leap. If it is falling far in front of you, the time to decide that you cannot reach it is after you have started for it at full speed. When you get close, you may see that it is too far away to take on the fly and you may then put on the brakes and play it on the bounce. But as long as there is even a faint chance that you will catch it, you should go after it. (There are special exceptions that will be discussed later.)

The outfielder does not stoop over for ground balls. He goes to one knee to stop them. If the ball goes past him, it is going to mean extra bases, even runs. Therefore, he must make *sure* it does *not* go through. He fields grounders like an infielder when runners are in scoring position and the score is close.

Willie Mays, outfielder for the San Francisco Giants, stretches for a high one.

The center fielder undoubtedly has the hardest fielding job, for the balls hit to center are the most difficult to judge. Coming straight off the bat, they sometimes seem to be ready to fall; then suddenly they "take off" over the fielder's head. Nothing but practice—practice at judging the flight of the ball and the sound of the bat hitting it—will enable you to beat this illusion.

Naturally, every outfielder covers as much ground to both right and left as he can. But the center fielder, with fair ground reaching out on both sides of him, has more potential coverage to provide.

When you play any position in the field you must learn to talk to your teammates. This is of prime importance in the outfield. Whenever you start toward the territory of another fielder to take a fly ball that is going to fall there, you should say, "I've got it!" And keep repeating it, until you hear him reply, "Take it!" If he has a better line on it, and it is a long run for you, he may shout you off. If he does, let him have it, and be sure to get out of his way as he comes toward you. Trot behind him and be ready to snag the ball if he muffs or misjudges it. Baseball is always a team game. Outfielders must learn to play together, to know each other's speed, and to call out their intentions to each other.

Sometimes the right fielder, who usually has the

sun in his eyes, may lose a ball in the sun. The center fielder, therefore, should give special attention
to fly balls going to his own left, and be ready to
move in on them if the right fielder asks him to.

There are times when a right fielder or left fielder
may not try to catch a fly ball. That usually occurs
when there is a runner on third with less than two
out, and the batter hits a long foul that will pull
the fielder far out of throwing position—make him
turn his back to the diamond to catch the ball
while going full speed away from the plate. Because
a caught fly means a chance for the runner to score
after the catch, the fielder may let such a foul fly
drop.

In the final inning, if the score is tied and the
home team gets a man on third with less than two
out, the fielders often trot in to play close behind
the infield, leaving the deep stretches of the outfield unguarded. They do this simply because a long
fly ball, under those circumstances, will win the
game whether the ball is caught or drops safely. (If
it is caught, the runner on third will be able to
score the winning run after the catch and the game
will be over.) What the fielders are guarding against
is the short blow over the infield—the single that
can bring in the winning run.

All outfielders must be able to throw, and know
when and where to throw. Before the game, the

Mickey Mantle (left) and Roger Maris. A good example of teamwork in the field.

outfielders should take time to warm up their arms. Even during a game, you will sometimes see big league fielders swinging their throwing arms around like a pitcher winding up. They are merely keeping their throwing muscles loose in case they have to try to nail a man at a base. Generally, the big league outfielder throws the ball a base ahead of the runner. But he must look at the runner and judge quickly if he has a base made or not. If he sees that a runner is but a stride away from second, he will throw to third. If the runner is rounding first, the outfielder will throw to second.

That is the safe way to play and the best way for young ballplayers. But an exceptional outfielder, like Mickey Mantle, with a strong and accurate arm, may play differently. If he sees a runner anticipating the routine throw to second, and making a wide turn at first base that takes him partially up the baseline to second base, he will occasionally rifle the ball to first to catch the runner off guard. That will work, however, only when the runner is loafing a bit on the baseline. If he is really pounding for second, such a throw will give him an extra base, so this play is used sparingly and only by fielders with throwing arms that are far better than average. The first baseman must be alerted to anticipate the throw.

John McGraw used to coach his outfielders in a

rally-killing play that used to surprise many base
runners. When batters start to pound the pitcher
with two base hits in a row, it is the conventional
practice for the fielders who recover the long hits
to heave the ball desperately for home. They do
this to try to nail the runner, who may have started
from second base. But McGraw's men would often
concede the run being made by the man who had
started from second and would instead rifle the ball
to second base. The runner on first, who might be
watching for the play at home, and who felt he
would get second base free while the ball was being thrown to the plate, would then be nailed flat-
footed. And the pitcher would have an easy out
with nobody left on base to worry about. This is
a good play for younger fielders who usually cannot get the ball home from the deep outfield without a relay.

In a big league game the outfielders should throw
the ball into the air with as little arc as possible
(throw a line drive) when throwing to the bases
unless there is a cut-off man. On throws from right
field to third base, for example, the cut-off man
would be the shortstop. When there is a cut-off
man, the ball should be thrown in the direction of
his head. In that way the cut-off man can catch
the ball if the third baseman sees that there is no
play at third and tells him to cut off the throw.

Unless the man attempting to score can bring in the decisive run in the game, the outfielder aims his throws to the plate at the cut-off man—the first baseman on throws from right and center field; the third baseman on throws from left field. The situation is handled in the same way as it is on throws from right field to third base. The catcher must determine whether he has a play at the plate and then must tell the cut-off man to let the ball go or to cut it off. If the winning run has a chance to score, the outfielder who has a strong enough arm should throw the ball on the fly all the way to the catcher at home plate, keeping the ball in the lowest possible arc. This kind of throw gets home faster and avoids bad bounces. Friction makes any ball that hits the ground slow down.

Willie Mays is noted for throwing line drives to home plate in order to catch runners attempting to score.

If the ball gets by one outfielder, the other two outfielders should get into the play. They have no bases to cover and it may take all three men to recover the ball quickly if it should bounce at an angle off the wall. And one outfielder may be needed to help relay the ball into the infield.

On any safe hit to the outfield, or any potentially safe hit, there is always an infielder who will run part way out in the grass to relay the ball in. He is the man to throw to if you are so far out that you cannot get the ball to the right base on one bounce. He knows where the ball should go since he is closer to the action. Do not make wild high throws to get the ball back into play. Get your eye on the relay man and rifle the ball into his hands. He may not get the batter out, but he will keep him from taking extra bases.

A good outfielder learns to play his own field. He studies the terrain and the bounces and the manner in which a ball rebounds from the wall. When Hank Greenberg, former Detroit slugger, switched from first base to the outfield to make room for another slugger (Rudy York) in the lineup, he spent hours learning to play his new position. Determined to improve his ability in the field, he asked a teammate to bounce balls off the outfield fence! Greenberg practiced going after them until he learned to judge at a glance just which way a ball would rebound. He worked at this hour after hour, even after everyone else had quit, until he became an able outfielder.

A young player should know that he cannot get ahead on his hitting alone. He should practice his fielding too, and he should get in the habit of playing as part of a team. He should always back up throws to a base, running in to be close enough to grab the ball if it should get past the baseman.

There are few sights harder to watch than a throw to second base bouncing away through center field, with no one near enough to retrieve the ball and to keep the runner from advancing. Even though an infielder may be backing up the throw too, an outfielder should get into position to stop the ball if it gets by everybody else. The right fielder backs up throws that come from the third-base side of the field to first or second, the left fielder backs up throws to third, and the center fielder moves in, even on an attempted steal, to save the throw if it gets away.

A good outfielder is a player who is constantly on the move. By positioning himself in accordance with the habits of the batter and the type of pitch the pitcher is throwing, he is able to make outs from well-hit balls. Connie Mack, who managed the Philadelphia team in the American League until he was over eighty, became famous for his constant shifting of fielders, using his scorecard as a signal. He would even alter the position of an outfielder if he thought his pitcher was losing a bit of his speed. He also had spots marked off (using the grandstand pillars as guides) for his fielders to move to in the late innings.

A young ballplayer does not often get a chance to become familiar with the hitting habits of the opposing batters. Still, if he sees that a batter is swinging late and he is playing the "opposite" field (right field for a right-handed batter), he can often get into a position to catch a blooping fly ball, just by playing a very short field.

An infielder must tell himself on every pitch that the ball is going to be hit to him, and he must know in advance exactly where he will throw the ball when it comes to him. He must be aggressive and confident. He should not merely hope that the ball does not come his way. Instead he should anticipate it, be ready for it, hope for it, and when the ball does come, he should move in on it as much as he can and watch it until it is safely in his glove.

The infielder, when he is fielding the ball, does not stoop. He squats. That is, he does not bend at the waist and reach down for the ball. He bends his knees and grabs the ball out in front of him. In the old days, infielders used to keep their heels together to keep a ball from going through. Now infielders crouch low with feet spread (about the width of their shoulders) and reach out for the ball, keeping their hands low and in front of the body. Taking the ball in the glove actually becomes automatic with practice, just as long as you *keep your eye on the ball.* In the beginning, you may flinch a little when the ball, especially if it is hit hard, comes close. But you must school yourself to keep your head down and your eyes on the ball. Then you will find that your hands move automatically to grab or stop it.

Coaches have a way of describing the efforts of a rookie to get in position to stop a ground ball. They say that he lets the ball play *him*. That is, he backs off and moves up and down, trying to get into the right spot. But a confident fielder (and only practice builds confidence) moves *toward* the ball and gets his hands out in front and down low to seize it. He cannot always wait for it to bounce properly, but grabs it wherever it is—on the short hop, at the top of a bounce, right on the ground. The short hop and the top of the bounce are the best places to catch it. If you keep your eye on the ball, you can glove it at any point, scooping the glove toward it and using your bare hand to help control it.

Although in some instances you may have to throw off balance to get the ball to the base ahead of the runner, usually you will have time to put him out with a strong throw. Top shortstops like Tony Kubek and Luis Aparicio always straighten up after fielding a ground ball hit to their right and fire a hard overhand throw to first base. The overhand throw with backspin in the ball gets there faster.

The shortstop is generally the busiest man in the

Luis Aparicio of the Baltimore Orioles is out at second in an attempted second inning steal. Aparicio was caught by Yankee catcher Elston Howard's throw to shortstop Tony Kubek.

infield, or at least the one who moves about most. The name "shortstop" originated in the very early days of baseball, when the pitching mound was fifteen feet closer to the plate, and there was far more room between the pitcher and the baseline. Then the shortstop ranged all around behind the pitcher to stop the short blows, while the outfielders took care of the long ones. Now the shortstop plays deep behind the baseline and often ranges into the short outfield to catch pop flies. He especially goes after balls that are falling behind third base—the ones that the third baseman has a hard time fielding.

The shortstop must have a strong arm for he must be able to go deep and far to his right to snag ground balls and still make the long throw to first base with plenty of power. But he must also act as a baseman to take throws and make put-outs at second base and (on rare occasions) at third. He must, when there is a runner on second, help to hold the runner close by bluffing a return to the bag to take a throw. This is an important part of his job and he should not neglect it because an easy score can be made if a base runner has a big lead off second base.

The second baseman and the shortstop have the job of putting the tag on a runner who is trying to steal. This is done by allowing the runner to slide into the ball. In a major league game, when a throw comes in to second, the man receiving the throw does not reach out to meet the runner. He quickly drops his gloved hand to the first base side of the bag and makes the runner put himself out. But he doesn't just hold the ball there and wait for the runner. He brush tags the runner and pulls the ball away as soon as possible. If the ball arrives too late for a brush tag, he grips the ball in both hands with the back of the glove toward the runner and attempts to get the ball between the runner and the base before the runner slides in safely. Without a tight grip on the ball, the impact of the runner sliding could knock the ball out of the infielder's hands.

One thing a shortstop (or a second baseman) does *not* do: He does not block off the base, stand between the base and the runner, or put even one foot there. When he makes his tag, he is behind the base, or partially straddling it, unless he is attempting a double play.

It is surprising how quickly young players can learn to make the double play—if they practice it properly. When the second baseman is the pivot man, he moves toward the base as quickly as possible, trying to arrive about a stride in back of the base as the ball is thrown by the shortstop. If the throw is on the outfield side of the base, he strides forward with his left foot as he catches the ball, pushing backward off the base with the left foot, pivoting on the right foot and throwing to first base.

If the throw from the shortstop is over or in front of the base, the second baseman strides forward, stepping on the base with his left foot, coming down on his right foot inside the base line, pivoting, and throwing to first base. When the throw is directly at the base, chest-high, many major league second basemen stay on the base, pushing off the base with the right foot as they throw directly down the base line to first base. Then they jump or roll to avoid the runner. However, there is a double danger in the "major league" play since the runner will slide into the pivot man and the throw may hit the runner. For this reason, the play is not recommended for young players.

When the shortstop is the pivot man on the double play, he also tries to time his arrival at second base so that he is a stride away from the base as the throw arrives. Then if the throw is on the inside of the diamond, he strides forward to meet the ball, his left foot comes down on the inside corner of the base, and he takes another stride to the inside of the base path, landing on his right foot as he throws to the first baseman.

If the throw is directly to the base or on the outfield side of the base, he brushes the outside corner of second base with his right foot as he strides forward, dragging the right foot past the base as he strides to the outfield side of the base with his left foot. Then he pushes off his right foot as he throws to first base to complete the double play.

It is better to make *one* sure out than to miss two, so the player should be sure to make the first out. Only after a player has had plenty of practice getting hold of the ball and throwing it accurately and strongly to first, should he begin to try double plays.

The shortstop is most often the man who runs out in the grass to take relays from left field and center field. He is also the cut-off man on throws from right field to third base. If a runner is heading for third on the throw-in, the third baseman may yell to the shortstop to let the throw come through. When that happens, the shortstop should leave the ball alone.

Like every other fielder, the shortstop should know what he is going to do even if the ball gets away from him. If it does, he should go after it without wasting a moment. All topnotch infielders scramble after the ball. The habit is so ingrained in them that it cannot be broken. Frankie Frisch, the Hall of Fame second baseman, once chased a muffed ground ball clear to the bleachers wall, although the game was over and there could be no play on it. Merely recovering the ball, however, is not enough.

Even as you pursue it, you must be planning where you will throw it.

Infielders have signals with each other to indicate which one will cover a base and to relay the catcher's call to the outfield. It helps a fielder to get a jump on the ball if he knows which way it may be hit—straight away if it is a fast ball, to the opposite field if it is a curve. Signals may be concealed from the opposition by giving them behind the back or behind the glove. Johnny Evers was one of the first infielders to signal his partner at short when he was to cover second. He did this by holding his glove up to his face and showing his open mouth or his bared teeth.

The second baseman does not have to make the long throws that the shortstop does, but he, too, must range widely to cover the base and to take ground balls on both sides. He frequently covers first base, when the first baseman has to charge in for a bunt. When the ball is hit to right field, the second baseman is the man who hurries out to the grass to take the relay. The catcher or another infielder will tell him, as he awaits the throw, whether he should turn and throw to third or relay the ball home.

The second baseman ranges to the right field foul line after pop flies, particularly when the right fielder is playing deep. He divides the work around second with the shortstop. When a throw comes to the shortstop from the direction of left field the second baseman backs up the throw. And when there is a runner on first and a ground ball goes to short, the second baseman is the pivot man on the double play.

The second baseman gets many slow-moving balls coming toward him, and he must charge them aggressively in order to get hold of them and to get the ball to first base in time. The throw, although short, is far from easy, and it takes much practice to learn to throw quickly across the body.

A good second baseman never concedes a safe hit. Bobby Richardson will sometimes knock down a hard-hit ball behind second base and still have time to pick it up and throw out the runner. Go after any ball you can reach and try to get your glove on it. If you can stop it from going through you may keep the batter from making extra bases.

The third baseman's spot is the hot corner, because he cannot afford to play too deep and yet he must field many hard-hit smashes. On hard-hit balls his first thought must be to stop the ball from going through. If he knocks it down, he often has time to pick it up, straighten his body, and slam the ball over to first in an overhand throw. He must have a strong arm for he has the longest distance to throw in the infield. And he should

Rocky Nelson of the Pittsburgh Pirates is an easy out at second base as Bobby Richardson of the New York Yankees waits with the ball in his glove.

have lightning reactions for often he must grab the ball and throw it in one motion. And, of course, he must know exactly where the ball should go.

Ordinarily, unless there is a clever bunter at bat, the third baseman plays well behind the baseline and not too close to the bag. He is never as deep as the shortstop and he must be a hog about running in front of the shortstop to nail any ground ball he can reach first. At the same time he must *always* be ready for a bunt. Notice the way an alert third baseman like Ken Boyer stays on his toes at all times while awaiting the pitch and the way he often begins to creep closer as the pitcher gets ready to deliver the ball. There are many batsmen in the leagues who will bunt any time they catch the third baseman "on his heels," for the baseman must get off the mark like a sprinter if he is going to pick up a baseline bunt and make the out at first. Whenever the batter squares away to bunt, the third baseman must start to sprint toward the plate. He does not wait for the pitcher to pitch. He must be off like a shot to give himself time for the play.

If you want to play third base, you must practice throwing from every position. And you must practice keeping your eyes on the ball until you have it firmly in your fingers.

Once in a while you must scoop up a bunt in

your bare hand and get it off to first in the same sweeping motion, but most of the time, you use two hands. The bare-hand play is a desperation play made by outstanding fielders.

If the bunt is on the baseline, you have to give it a chance to roll foul. Once it does, brush it quickly away, so it will not roll fair again. And *never* let a seemingly foul bunt roll past you.

At third base you should never get in front of the bag to take throws. Straddle the bag, so that you can reach right or left for the throw, and put the tag on close to the bag. Or if it is a force-out, requiring no tag, stretch toward the ball as the first baseman does.

In the late innings of a tight ball game, the third baseman should move closer to the foul line so he can stop any ground ball that goes between him and the line. A ground ball that gets by on that side of him will be an extra base hit, and such a blow may cost his team the ball game. A ground ball that gets by on his left side will be a single.

The first baseman is usually considered the in-fielder who has the least need for fielding skill. It is true that a few awkward players have played first base in the majors almost entirely on the strength of their batting. But a first baseman is in a position to do his team serious damage if he does not develop some skill at covering the bag. He must also be ready to charge the plate on a bunt so that a sacrifice won't become a base hit.

Most first basemen are tall and left-handed. Their height enables them to reach high and wide for throws. And left-handers can get a throw off to another base without having to turn their backs to the diamond. Yet one of the best-fielding first basemen of recent years is Vic Power, who is right-handed both at the bat and in the field. His great skill as a fielder more than compensates for his need to shift his feet around to get set for a throw to second.

The chief job of the first baseman, and the one that occupies most of his time, is catching throws to the base to put out the runner. In taking these throws he must be ready to reach to either side or to stretch toward the throw on a close play so that he will glove it more quickly. But in order to make the out, he must have his foot in contact with the base. More than 90% of the plays are made with the same foot on the base: the left foot if you throw left-handed, and the right foot if you throw right-handed.

In stretching toward the throw, as all good first basemen do when the play looks reasonably close, the idea is to get as long a stride as possible. You will often see Power practically do a split to get all the distance he can. Naturally you step forward

with the left foot if you are catching the ball in the left hand, and with the right if you are taking it in the right hand. The foot on your throwing side is kept in contact with the base. Your *toe* should be on the base when you start your stretch. If you try to keep contact with your heel, your

stretch is bound to pull your heel off the bag and the runner will be safe. This stretch is another move you must practice. A first baseman who does not reach toward the throw is doing only seventy-five per cent of his job. Years ago the Yankees let a first baseman go because he had "short arms." This means that he had a habit of taking the throws with a bent elbow so that he did not have the advantage of a full stretch.

Because many of the throws to first are made off balance, the first baseman must be ready to reach in every direction and to dig them out of the dirt on either side. Many throws must be taken backhanded, with the hand turned over, thumb-down on the "wrong" side of the body. Taking throws this way is not difficult if you make up your mind that the ball can be caught; if you do not try to keep your body facing the throw while you reach across; and if you keep your eye on the ball. Turn naturally, with the foot that is on the side of your glove hand stepping right out along with the glove —even if you must partially turn your back toward the man who threw the ball—and watch the ball right into the glove. If you have difficulty doing this, have someone throw balls to your "wrong" side and practice backhand catches.

If a throw is really wild, and you are not going to be able to stretch to it, leave the bag at once and stop the throw at all costs. It is better to concede the base than to lose the ball.

The first baseman plays as far off the base as he can, but not so far that he cannot get back to take the throw. If you straddle the bag and wait for the throw, you are not playing far enough off the bag.

You should have just time enough to sprint back to the bag, find it with your *toe* (the left toe for left-handed players), then turn toward the infielder who is fielding the ball. If you must shift feet, make the shift quickly with a little hop. And get your *toe* on the inside of the bag.

Only in blocking low throws do you shift your feet at first base to get your body in front of the ball. A left-handed first baseman will shift feet on a low throw into the dirt to his left so that his body will be in front of the ball and have a chance to block it. A right-handed first baseman will shift feet on a low throw to his right to get his body in front of the ball.

When holding a man on the bag, a good first

baseman does not put his foot on the baseline. He places his right foot on the home side of the base. When he receives the throw, he sweeps his glove hand back and down, close to the bag, so that the runner will run or slide into it. Major leaguers almost never concede that a runner has gotten back to the base safely. They will always put the tag on him if they can, for every now and then a man may overslide the bag by just a little and can be caught with his foot off it.

When the first baseman walks in to talk to the pitcher, he is often telling him how he plans to play in case of a bunt. The pitcher needs to know if the baseman is going to leave the bag, for the pitcher often has to cover. The pitcher will also run over to make the put-out when the first base-man has fielded the ball any distance from the bag. Then the baseman throws the ball underhand, if the distance is relatively short, or overhand, if he has gone far to his right to field the ball. He aims about chest-high so it will be easy for the pitcher to handle it as he reaches first base.

When fly balls are hit to right field and center field, the first baseman must be ready to cut off a throw to home plate and make a throw to second.

There are general fielding secrets that infielders and outfielders share. One of these has to do with fielding fly balls close to the fence. Whenever it is

Bobby Richardson races to catch a fly ball.

possible to judge that a fly ball is going to the fence or just beyond it, a good fielder runs to the fence *first*, then moves along the fence to make the catch. Also, most fielders try to catch fly balls with their hands high so that they can get a throw off quickly. When the throw is going to be long and must be sent off fast (when a fast runner is on third on a not-too-deep fly ball) Mickey Mantle will deliberately slow his approach to the ball so that he can catch it on the run and have the added momentum of the run to put power into his throw. But the important thing is to catch the ball.

All fielders, at one time or another, are likely to lose a fly ball in the sun. That is why all fielders have sun glasses which they can flip down when they need to look up into the sun. A big leaguer never looks directly into the sun without sunglasses, for he knows that this can blind him for several seconds.

Here are the major points for infielders and out-fielders to bear in mind:

1. Keep your eyes on the ball when you are fielding a grounder. Never be caught with your chin up.

2. Charge a slow-moving ball to take it at the top of the bounce or on the pick-up.

3. Straighten up and throw overhand for accuracy on balls hit to your right.

4. Do not stoop for ground balls. Crouch down to get near them.

5. Do not stand on a baseline without the ball.

6. Outfielders: Practice going back for fly balls to take them over the shoulder.

7. Know the field and where all obstacles are.

8. Move fast to get into every play, to back up throws, or to cover open bases.

Base Running

5

The first thing a big league manager tells his charges about running bases is to touch the bases on the *inside.* A big leaguer does not step squarely on a base when he is rounding it, for that makes the run longer and slows the runner down. There is also the risk of twisting an ankle if the spikes on the runner's shoes catch in the bag. Little Leaguers do not wear spikes, so they are not likely to twist an ankle if they step on the base. But this big league habit of touching bases on the inside is a good one to form right from the start.

A player must also learn the technique of sliding.

The slide is just a controlled fall. When it was first used, it was either a head-first plunge or a sudden sitting-down to skid into the base, feet first. Sliding head first is the easiest, but it is also the most dangerous, for it causes many head, shoulder, and arm injuries. It should be used only in returning to a base. A man taking a big lead off a base must sometimes plunge back head first when he is caught leaning the wrong way.

More and more big league base runners are using the "straight-in" or "bent-leg" slide, in which one leg is bent under so that the body slides along with the weight on the shin of the bent leg. The upper part of the leg is aimed straight at the base, with the knee slightly lifted. The foot makes the first contact with the bag. There are two advantages to this slide: The runner is able to rise to his feet simply by straightening out the bent leg; and he reaches the base more quickly.

The "hook" slide is still used to avoid a tag at any base. In this slide, the body weight is carried on one thigh and the top leg is bent slightly with the foot extended so that it hooks the base on the way by.

Whenever you slide, you should lift both hands in the air to avoid the danger of twisting a wrist under your weight or of jamming a finger on the ground. Most good base runners have a habit that is worth imitating. If you watch a fast runner at first, you will see that he picks up dirt in each hand and holds on to it. He is not just drying off his hands, nor is this a nervous habit. He holds on to the dirt to remind himself to throw his hands in the air when he slides.

Like most baseball skills, sliding requires confidence, and it is constant practice that builds confidence. Sliding on grass, without wearing spikes, is the easiest and safest way to practice.

A base runner, whether he plans to steal or not, must always take as big a lead as the opposition will allow. When you practice, you will learn how far you can wander from the bag and still have time to get back safely in case of a throw. Do not leave yourself too wide a margin. Take as much of a lead as you can get, or as much as you think you can take. But don't go so far that you can't plunge back if you are caught. Usually the length of your body plus a step is what you can take. If you have good speed, you may dare to take a little more to force the pitcher to pay attention to you.

The base runner at second base usually watches the second baseman and allows the third-base coach to watch the shortstop. Ordinarily the runner can afford to get as far off the base as the infielder is, but he plunges back quickly if the infielder darts for the bag or if the coach shouts, "Get back!"

Willie Davis of the Los Angeles Dodgers slides into third base . . .

. . . and touches the bag just in time.

The umpire ruled him safe.

When the ball is pitched, the runner always runs a few steps toward the next base, then reverses quickly if the ball is not hit.

If the ball is hit in the air you can often judge if there is a chance of its being caught. Then you will know whether you should take off, tag up, or just move half way down the baseline and watch —ready to run if the ball is dropped.

Major league ball players seldom drop fly balls, yet the base runners always move down the baseline prepared to take advantage of such an error. But they usually know the throwing ability of the outfielders they face, and they take that into account as they move up the baseline. In amateur baseball, fly balls are dropped more often, and it is important for a runner to be ready at all times to run on an error.

No big league base runner ever takes a lead off third base except in foul territory. He does not move down the baseline but down the grass outside the baseline. This is simply to avoid the danger of being hit by a fair ball and put out. He knows that the only batted ball that can hit him when he is on the grass has to be foul. On the other lines he must, of course, try to avoid being hit, but occaionally a big league base runner will deliberately slow down a bit to pass in front of an infielder just before the ground ball gets there. He does this

Vic Power of Minnesota slides safely into home plate with a stolen base. John Romano, Cleveland catcher, tries for tag but is too late.

merely to add to the infielder's difficulties. But it is a dangerous practice, and should be used only by a runner who has excellent judgment and good speed. Unless there is a "force play" situation, the base runner doesn't advance on a ball that is hit in front of him. If there is no runner on first base, but there is a runner on second base and the ball is hit to the shortstop, the runner on second doesn't attempt to advance to third base.

In order to score after the catch of a sacrifice fly, the base runner must be off at the earliest possible moment. But if he starts too soon, he will set himself up for an easy double play. So the runner must watch and start the moment the ball touches the fielder's glove. The runner always has his foot in contact with the base and is ready to take off

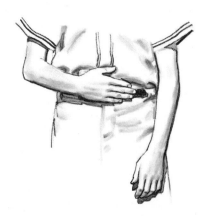

like a sprinter. As he approaches home, the on-deck batter is the man for him to watch, for the batter will give him the signal to slide or to come in standing up. When the batter holds his hand up, as if in a stop signal, he is telling the runner to stay up. When he puts his hands palm down, he is telling him to slide *fast!* Runners are told to slide only to avoid a tag because they can always run faster than they can slide and at home plate they don't have to stay on the base.

The baseline coaches are the traffic cops for the base runners. But many of their signals are given in code—a code they hope only their own players will understand. Big league coaches, particularly the coach at third base, give many signs—gesturing with the hands, hitching the belt, adjusting the cap—to

pass on to the hitter or the runner, or both, the orders that come from the bench. But they also give simple signals that base runners have to watch for and obey. When a coach does not want a runner to advance, he will hold up both hands in a stop sign. When he wants him to come on but not go past the base, he may hold up one hand and give a "come-on" sign with the other, meaning: "This is your base, but make your turn." And when he gestures vigorously, palms down, he means: "It's going to be close! Slide!" Of course when he wants the runner to turn and keep going, he gives a generous "come-on" sign with his arm.

When a runner is going from second to third base, he must watch the coach and obey his signals. In going from first to second, the runner is often in a better position than the coach to see what is happening in the field or on the baselines ahead of him. The good base runners never fail to keep an eye on the outfielders who are trying to field the ball. Several of the best base runners have adopted this system: If the ball gets away on the glove-side of the fielder, they will try for the extra base. They know that when the fielder catches up with the ball, he will not be in a position to make an immediate throw. Of course if the ball is in the outfielder's hands as they make their turn around the base, they know that they cannot advance unless the ball is so far out that it must be relayed in. This is another time when it helps to know the fielder's throwing ability.

An alert base runner always watches to see if the base ahead of him is covered, or if there is a fielder closer to the base than he is. Even in the big leagues, infielders will sometimes become confused and leave a base unguarded. Whenever you have a chance to reach a base before a fielder can get there, the base is yours, unless a teammate is already there.

The strategy of big league base running and the defenses against it have changed in recent years. Many of the plays the old-timers used to employ are not seen any more. For instance, in the early days of baseball, the team managers (called "captains" then) used to tell the base runners that the way to steal a base was to stand idly near the base and try to look as if they had no intention of advancing. But nowadays, the alert runner tries to make the pitcher believe he is likely to advance on any pitch. He takes a generous lead, bends forward to watch the pitcher, and sometimes turns and pretends to dig hard for second, when he really plans to take only a step or two.

When the base runner does start for second, he takes his first step with either foot, whichever is most natural, and goes all out for the base. He

never glances back to see if the catcher has un-
leashed his throw, and he tries to slide in on the
opposite side of the base from the man who is taking the throw.

Many years ago, base runners would sometimes
steal bases by breaking for second just as the
catcher tossed the ball back to the pitcher. Today,
big leaguers do not *toss* the ball back to the pitcher
when there is a man on base. They snap it back
hard and fast. But some amateur catchers still toss
the ball back lazily. When this happens it is still
possible for a base runner who has a good enough
lead to steal a base.

Now a big league base runner steals on the
pitcher. He makes a close study of a pitcher's moves
so that he can tell when the pitcher has finally
committed himself to pitch to the plate and will
not turn to catch the runner off base. Maury Wills,
the best base stealer in the leagues, never fails to
study the pitchers on the other clubs. Between times
at bat, he sits on the bench and gets a teammate to
judge him as he decides just when it would be best
to run. Maury will watch the pitcher stretch, pause,
check the runner, and get ready to pitch. Then he
says, "Now!" to indicate when he would start for
second if he were the runner. The teammate will
then tell him either, "You got it!" or "No, he'd
have nailed you." This "game" helps Maury recog-

nize the telltale move or pose that indicates when and where the pitcher is going to pitch.

A player as talented as Maury Wills is usually allowed to steal whenever a base is unoccupied and he thinks he can make it. But most players must watch for a signal from the third-base coach or listen for one from the first-base coach. There are a dozen different moves a coach can make to signal a steal: the skin-to-skin sign (the bare hand touched to bare skin), the skin-to-cloth sign (the bare hand rubbed on cloth), the covered belt-buckle, two hands on the cap, and many others. Some coaches give signals with their feet, either by putting one foot outside the coaching box, by walking toward the batter, or by backing away. Or the coach may cup his hands to shout something to the batter or runner: "Look alive!" or "Get a good one!" Then the sign would depend on whether he cups his hand around both mouth and nose or just around the mouth.

Invariably, however, there is one special sign to indicate that a signal is coming. Otherwise the opposition would be sure to steal the signal. The coach may run through his whole category of signs when only one of them is "alive." The sign that the live signal is coming can be a special pose (arms folded, hands on knees, fist in air); or it may be a vocal signal, such as calling the player by his last name instead of by his nickname. Then the coach may give one of the standard signs, which will be the right one, to be followed by half a dozen others which are meaningless. The batter or base runner must be careful not to betray by his reaction that the live sign has been given. He should keep his eyes on the coach even after the sign has been flashed; he must watch the meaningless signs, too. Then he can indicate that he has received the sign by a return signal—kicking the base twice, shifting his bat, picking up dirt in one hand.

It is necessary to indicate only that the sign has been received in plays that require the cooperation of two players. Every big league batter has a hit-and-run sign of his own that he gives to the runner on base. The runner must then have a way of indicating that he has the sign and will be off with the pitch.

There are, of course, standard hit-and-run situations when the runner needs no sign. For example, with two men out and a full count on the batter, everyone starts running with the pitch. Occasionally a major league manager will get his base runners moving together, even when the count is not full and there are less than two out. A double steal is sometimes called to move runners when runs are desperately needed and there is no long-ball hitter coming up. When there are two men stealing, an effort is often made to draw a throw to one so the other can take off for home. In such instances, the runner nearest home is the important man and he must be protected even if it means the other runner goes out.

Sometimes a base runner is caught in a run-down and then he will try to stay "alive" long enough for the other runner to advance. He does this by dodging back and forth, away from the fielder who has the ball. The opposition is always trying to run him back to the base farthest from the plate. And sometimes a runner can escape by bluffing—moving with a false step toward the man who has the ball, then scurrying back toward the other base, then bluffing again, before the pursuing fielder throws. Then the runner takes a few more steps until he has gained enough distance to be able to make it back in one long dive. But if there is another runner trying to advance, the trapped runner keeps away from the tag as long as possible.

Ty Cobb believed that "the baseline belongs to the runner." A defensive man without the ball has no right to block the baseline either. And even if a catcher awaits the runner with the ball in his hand, the big league runner sometimes piles right into him and knocks the ball loose. It is safer and

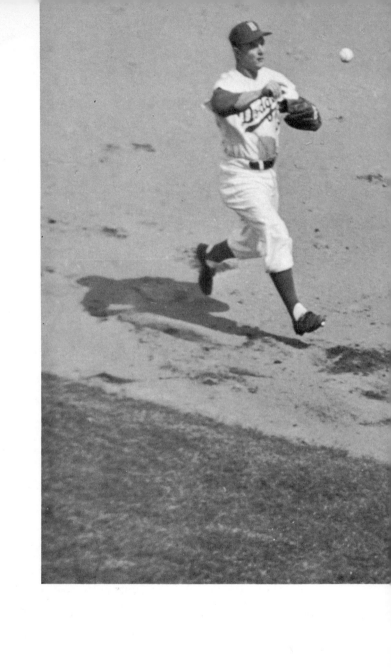

Chico Fernandes of the Philadelphia Phillies tries to return to first base as Brooklyn Dodgers' catcher, Roy Campanella, and shortstop, Don Zimmer (left), run him down.

Vic Wertz of the Cleveland Indians falls away as he starts to slide to avoid tag by Giants' Hank Thompson.

more effective, however, to slide away from the tag, past the plate, and then to hook the plate with one toe or to reach back to it with one hand.

Ballplayers in the big leagues do a great deal of running—not only to practice base stealing but also to keep their muscles in shape.

Here then, are your big league tips for base running and stealing:

1. Touch bases on the inside corner.
2. Keep your hands in the air when sliding.
3. Lead off third base in foul territory.
4. Go for any base that is unguarded.
5. Slide away from a baseman who holds the ball.
6. Study the pitcher carefully to find telltale signs that will give you a jump.
7. Obey the coach but do not give away his signs.
8. Stay alive in a run-down to give the other runner a chance.
9. Keep your legs in shape by running.

Winning Ball Games

6

A big league manager generally tries to win a game "big" in the first five innings. After that he is satisfied if he wins the game at all. Because almost every big league team carries its quota of long-ball hitters who can drive in several runs at a blow, the strategy in the first half of a baseball game is to try for the "big inning." For that reason, the manager will seldom make use of the bunt or the steal, except in instances where the percentages strongly favor that move. He will be satisfied instead to get his men on base in the hope that one of his sluggers will come to bat with potential runs ahead of him and be able to drive them all in at once. He will use the bunt only when his pitcher (or another feeble hitter) comes up to bat with a man on first and less than two out. He will order the steal only when a real speedster is on base.

He will, however, frequently order the hit-and-run if he has a man on first and the batter can "get ahead" of the pitcher—that is, work the count to two balls and no strikes, or three balls and one strike. If the batter is left-handed, so that it is easier for him to hit behind the runner, the manager is more likely to order the hit-and-run. And if the pitcher is right-handed—which makes it easier for the left-handed batter to hit the ball and easier for the runner to take a lead—the percentages are improved in favor of working the hit-and-run play successfully.

In amateur baseball, these percentages are very different and so it is not often possible to use the same strategy. Many amateur teams have no long-ball hitter at all, or only one, and so they have little chance of building a big inning with long base hits alone. There are other percentages to figure on in the lesser leagues and so although the tactics may differ, the basic plan of "playing the percentages" can still be employed.

For instance, in many school leagues and in some Little League baseball, fielding and throwing are not good. Therefore the percentages are in the batter's favor if he can just get the ball in fair territory on the ground, where it must be fielded and thrown. So runs can often be fashioned very quickly with the help of bunts and chops, combined with alert base running. Under such circumstances, especially if he is working with a weak-hitting team, even a big league manager would decide that he should try every way he can to bring in whatever runners happen to get on base. Even in the first inning, he would use a bunt to move a runner from first to second or from second to third. If he got a man to third base with less than two out, the chances are good, too, that he would use a squeeze play to bring him in. Lacking strong hitters, he would find the percentages in his favor only if he could get the batter to hit the ball on the ground to move the runners—yet not hit it so that it reached an infielder too soon. He would order bunts and chops to keep his base runners moving, and would probably have his runners steal whenever they could get a good lead.

At the beginning of any game, a major league batter tries to get a line on the pitcher who is facing him. Sometimes a batter, waiting on deck as the pitcher takes his warm-up throws, will be seen swinging his bat as the warm-up pitch comes to the plate. In this way, even from several feet away, he tries to time the pitcher's delivery.

At the plate, in the first few innings, the hitters will usually "take" the first pitch, just to get a line on what the pitcher is throwing and how fast he is. If the pitcher in his warm-ups or in pitching to earlier batters seems to have trouble with his control, it is a good practice for most batters to let the first pitch go by.

When the count runs to three balls and no strikes or to three balls and one strike, the big leaguer will almost always take the next pitch in the hope that he will get a walk. (Only when there are runs in scoring position, or when the batter is a powerful hitter who does not often get a good pitch, will the manager give the batter the sign to hit the "cripple" pitch—the 3 and 0 pitch—if it looks good to him.) In amateur ball waiting out the pitcher is even more important, if he is at all wild. When waiting out the pitcher, the batter does not just slump at the plate and watch the ball go by. It is more upsetting to the pitcher if the batter seems ready to hit. Sometimes, when the count has gone to three balls, a batter will square around as if to bunt, just as the pitcher is ready to deliver, thus distracting his view of the target. However, too much movement also makes it difficult for the umpire to judge the pitch and he may give the benefit of the doubt to the pitcher.

A big league manager and his coaches spend a great part of their time searching out the weaknesses of the opposition. They watch an outfielder to see how he throws and to see if he has a sore arm that he is favoring—a weakness they can take advantage of during the ball game. They study the moves of the pitcher and the catcher to see if there is any difference in their behavior when a fast ball is thrown, and when a curve ball is thrown. And of course they make a special study of the hitters to see the pitches they like best and to what part of the field they hit.

When there are only two or three chances to see the same team in action, such study is not possible. But even during a game, you can use big league methods to get a line on the other players. If you find a right-handed batter who habitually swings late, you can often get him out by playing your right fielder close to the foul line. Many late swinging batters do not get any power into their hits, so you can shorten up on them considerably in the field. If they hit a fly ball, it will most likely drop not far behind first base, or behind the baseline from first to second. And if the outfielder is playing shallow, he can run quickly to grab the ball on the fly. Even if the ball is hit on a line, the outfielder, playing shallow, can sometimes take the drive on the first hop and throw the man out at first. Inexperienced players sometimes concede themselves a single on such blows and do not sprint to first. Play like this would not be possible in the big leagues of course. But it is applying the big league "percentage" methods to the league that you are playing in.

Often when an announcer is describing a big league ball game, he will say that the infield is at "double-play" depth and is conceding a run. A manager will instruct his team do this when he is holding a good lead or when the game is young and he would rather trade a run for two outs than let the other side develop a big inning. When the infield moves in to make ready for a throw to home plate, soft line drives and even high bounders sometimes get through for extra bases. The "double-play" depth is "playing for the outs"—forgetting about the base runners and playing back far enough to field the ground balls comfortably and get the runners on the force plays.

Infielders as well as outfielders should be prepared to move according to the percentages. Of course, first basemen and second basemen usually play deep when a strong left-hander is at bat. In the big leagues, when a confirmed pull-hitter is up, the manager of the defensive team sometimes uses an exaggerated shift in the infield that may put the shortstop between first and second, or right behind second base. Such exaggerated shifts are not often necessary in amateur ball. But fielders can still be played far out of their traditional position when you know the type of hit the batter usually makes. A confirmed "straight-away" hitter can sometimes be put out by letting the second baseman play almost on top of second base, ready to cut off a hard blow over the bag. Sometimes a late-swinging left-hander can be outwitted by having the third baseman move back a step and stay near the baseline, instead of moving toward the shortstop position as he normally would.

There are many situations in which the defensive team is certain of the offense's next move. With the pitcher at bat, a man on first, and less than two out, a bunt is fairly certain unless the team at bat is far behind. Therefore, you will see big league infielders all move with the pitch in case of a bunt, in the hope that they may get the ball soon enough to put the lead runner out—spoiling the whole maneuver. Both the first baseman and the third baseman will break toward the plate as soon as the pitcher starts to throw. The pitcher, too, as soon as he has pitched the ball, will come down off the mound quickly and move toward the batter. The shortstop will move to cover second base, while the second baseman will move toward first. Every now and then, such strategy will result in a double play: a neatly fielded bunt, a hard throw to second, and a rifling of the ball to first. But that is just an extra dividend. The real aim of the play is to get the runner at second. If that does not seem possible, if the runner has got too good a jump to be thrown out, the ball must be snapped to first to get the batter out.

Although pitchers in the big leagues, under those circumstances, sometimes make the pitch hard to bunt, it is often just as well to let the man bunt rather than to get the pitcher in a hole so that he must groove a pitch. Even when a bunt is obvious, it may sometimes be "taken off" if the batter gets far ahead of the pitcher. A walk, after all, is even better than a sacrifice bunt.

But when the squeeze play seems in order—when there is a man on third, one out, the winning or tying run on third, and a practiced bunter at bat—the pitcher may try hard to keep the batter from bunting. A ball thrown high and inside is not easy for a batter to bunt and often will produce a little pop fly that can lead to two quick outs. On the squeeze play, the pitcher must follow his pitch in quickly and be ready to field the ball and flip it home without delay.

Among inexperienced ballplayers the squeeze play is sometimes unusually productive. Again it is a matter of "percentages." The pitcher, or whichever player fields the ball, may be concentrating so intently on getting the man at the plate that when he misses him he may think only of making the "easy out" at first and will do that deliberately. That is in accordance with the percentages at least, for young ballplayers do not often think two plays ahead. But if you have a man on second and a man on third with only one out, or none out, and if the pitcher, concentrating on the runner at third, allows the man at second to get a good long lead, it may be possible to bring *both* men in on the squeeze. The runner at second need only break for third as soon as the man ahead of him breaks for home. When the second man rounds third base, he can tell in an instant where the ball is going to be thrown. If the pitcher hesitates a second before he fires the ball to first, the charging runner from second will have an excellent chance of getting home safe.

In the big leagues the manager will not often allow such situations to develop. If he can afford it (that is, if it is not a matter of putting the winning run on base in the late innings), he will not leave first base open. He will walk the batter to create a force play at every base, and make it easier to put a man out at the plate—inasmuch as the catcher need not tag the runner.

Intentional walks are given only when the percentages are in their favor—when the winning run is in scoring position, a dangerous slugger is at bat, first base is open, and a weak hitter is coming up next. Occasionally an intentional walk may be given as part of a complicated strategy—to force the other manager, or merely to tempt him, to send in a pinch hitter for the pitcher and thus to get an effective pitcher out of the game. By walking the man ahead of the pitcher, with the winning run on second, the defensive team may make it seem worthwhile to the other team to seize the opportunity of bringing the big run in.

But the percentages change when there is uncertainty about fielding or batting skills. It is not often good percentage baseball in Little League or school ball to give a batter an intentional walk, unless it is done to set up a force play at home. Double plays just do not occur frequently enough to make the risk worthwhile. And the frequency of fielding errors gives every base runner a chance to make a potential run.

There is one type of double play, however, that is performed by some semi-skilled players. It is called the "trapped ball" double play, and is one of the earliest bits of fielding strategy in the game. An easy fly ball is deliberately dropped in the infield when there is a runner on first. This immediately creates a force play at second base and, because the runner sticks close to first awaiting the "certain" out on the fly, there is no rush to get the ball there. So many young batters surrender on a fly ball of this type that the relay to first need not be hurried either. The rules prevent the use of this trick when there are two on base (including first). The real trick is to keep the ball under control without catching it first and then dropping it. If it just hits the flat glove and drops in front of the fielder, it can be retrieved and thrown easily, without dangerous haste.

When giving out walks, even intentionally, amateur ballplayers sometimes forget what every big leaguer knows: Even on the fourth ball, the ball is still "alive." Although the batter's base running is automatic and he may take first base without being put out, there is no rule that says he must stop at first. On the contrary, if the ball gets past the catcher and the catcher fails to scramble after it, the batter should sprint to first and make his turn, ready to take second if the catcher has not recovered the ball.

On a third strike, too, if first base is empty, the batter can take whatever he can get, if the strike gets by the catcher. A big league batter, with two strikes on him, may deliberately swing at a wild pitch that is obviously going to escape the catcher. Even big leaguers sometimes overlook the fact that if the third strike hits the dirt in front of the plate, the batter may still try for first. And occasionally a smart ballplayer will swing at such a pitch and get to first before the catcher (who may actually have stopped the ball) realizes that the strikeout is not complete. The catcher doesn't have to hold the third strike for a put-out in Little League baseball.

Making the right kind of turn at first base is a simple matter that is sometimes neglected. A big league base runner who is going to make the turn for second starts to make it before he gets to first. He runs into foul territory before he reaches the bag so that he can touch the inside corner of the base as he swings in a short arc toward second. Too wide a swing or too late a turn will cost time and may cost the base. The runner should run the last half of the distance from home plate to first base in the "three-foot" lane. If you are running on a passed ball, you can count on the coach to tell you if you should try for second.

Teamwork in baseball requires constant communication among players and between coach and player. Games are sometimes lost by failure to work as a team. When the pitcher runs in to field a bunt, the catcher must tell him what to do with the ball when he gets it, for the catcher can see the play and the pitcher cannot.

When a big league second baseman scoots out

Milwaukee Braves shortstop, Johnny Logan, was right under this fly ball but it was caught by outfielder Wes Covington (left).

into right field after a soft liner or pop fly, he listens to what the outfielders tell him. If one of them warns him off the ball, the baseman gives up on it. But he cannot afford to watch the outfielders first to see if they need his help. He starts for the ball at once and relies on his mates to tell him what to do.

Strategy in a big league game may shift from inning to inning. The team that is six runs behind plays an entirely different game from the team that is several runs ahead. The team that has a lead starts to build that lead one run at a time: bunting, stealing, trying for the extra base. The team that is far behind plays it safe at every base. It must conserve its outs in the hope of starting a big inning. Bunting a single run to scoring position is of little value when five or six runs are needed. So the batters will hit away, even at the risk of a double play, in the exact situation that would have called for a bunt earlier in the game.

Many teams routinely "take off" the bunt sign when the count has gone to two strikes and a foul bunt will put the batter out. But when the man at bat is a hopeless hitter—a pitcher with a low average—the big league manager will often decide that the man may as well bunt out as strike out, and he will let him keep on trying to drop a bunt into fair territory.

In a crucial short series—the World Series, for instance—strategy may also alter radically. In such a series, a manager cannot afford to "save" players for games that may never be played, or to keep a weak hitter in the line-up so that he may provide strong defense in an inning that may never come. You do not send a weak hitter up in the ninth inning, with the winning run in scoring position, because you think that hitter will be useful in checking the opposition later on. "Later on" may be too late.

The home team in the big leagues can afford to play for a tie, because they always have a last chance to win, no matter what the score. But the visiting team must play to win, and must play to win by as many runs as possible, even in the top of the ninth with the score tied. That means that the visiting manager has got to pour all his best troops into the battle. All the great major league managers have been men who have played to win the game of the day and who have always been ready to gamble.

Deception does not play as great a part in baseball as it used to. When it was still an amateur game, played more for love than money, the players were advised to try to conceal their intent at all times—to stand at the base as if they had no idea of stealing, to idle at the plate as if they did not mean to swing. Then, later, managers like Connie Mack and Clark Griffith began to think up schemes to outwit the umpires as well as the opposition. This was especially true in the days when one umpire, whose back was often turned to part of the play, had to handle the whole game.

Now it is considered "bush-league" to try to fool an umpire by childish tricks. But players must be alert to keep their opponents from fooling them. The hidden ball trick, once fairly common in the major leagues, is hardly ever used any more, for coaches and players are all trained to keep watch on the ball and take nothing for granted. And the rules prevent the pitcher from taking his position on the rubber when he does not have the ball. The deception now consists of working illusions on base runners by pretending to field balls that cannot be fielded, or pretending that a throw is not coming when it is on the way. Every now and then, a catcher will take a runner unawares by standing with his hands on his hips when the throw is almost upon him, making the runner think that he has plenty of time to coast home without sliding.

A shortstop or a second baseman can sometimes decoy a runner into stopping at second by pretending to field a ground ball that is really out of reach and is going through to the outfield. And a few outfielders have been able to lure base runners into running by pretending to watch a ball over the fence, when they really were ready to take the ball on the fly. This trick tempts the runners to go so far from their bases that they become easy victims of a double play. But it takes supreme confidence and excellent judgment to work these illusions.

A simpler trick that some base runners use is to draw a throw by pretending to keep going past a base where you really intend to stop. It is good practice, especially among younger players, to draw a throw whenever you can. But you do need good judgment to know how far past a base you can move and still return safely.

However, a ball player increases his value to his team only by perfecting his skills. A pitcher must work constantly on his control, pitching to smaller and smaller targets as his judgment grows sharper. A batter practices hitting the pitches he finds hardest to hit. An infielder works on the difficult stops and plays. A catcher needs to practice his throws until he can get one off quickly to any base.

Outfielders, in order to strengthen their arms, are always careful to take a step when they throw, even if they are just playing catch. And as they grow more skilled at judging the flight of fly balls, they practice taking the ball over the shoulder of the throwing arm, so they can save even a split second in getting the ball back into the field.

Every player trains himself for the part he must play when he does not field the ball himself. Big league managers give black marks to rookies who fail to back up bases on throws (they back up as far as possible—at least 20 to 30 feet), or who do not run out to take relays when they should, or who fail to get into position to cut off throws from the outfield.

There are always one or two superstars who can get by as just hitters and a number of pitchers who can do nothing but pitch. But the men who have lasted in the leagues are those who have played the game as it was meant to be played, as a team game, with each player trying to synchronize his moves with those of his teammates and trying to help them do their own jobs better.

Here, then, are the general rules for playing winning baseball:

1. Play the percentages, or the probabilities, of your own league. Where fielding is ragged and batting spasmodic, do not try to work complicated plays or plays that call for the accurate placing of hits. Concentrate on hitting line drives. Give the opposition a chance to make errors. Always look for the extra base.

2. Look for weaknesses in the opposition, and take advantage of them.

3. Have your pitcher pitch outside to a man

who habitually steps away from the pitch and inside to a batter who crowds the plate. Have him pitch high to a man who takes overlong strides.

4. Take extra bases on the outfielder who cannot throw. Steal on the catcher who must take extra steps to get his throws off.

5. Suit your tactics to the situation. Play to tie in the late innings, or in overtime, when you are the home team. Play to win when you are the visiting team. Build a lead one run at a time. Play it safe when you need a lot of runs.

6. Play position on the enemy batters. Remember late-swingers hit to the "opposite" field.

7. Learn the rules. A third strike must be "fairly caught"—that is, *before* it hits the ground—or the batter can run. In the Little League, however, the third strike doesn't have to be caught for the batter to be out. A fourth ball is "alive."

8. Talk to your teammates and listen to them. Never wait for the other fellow to catch a ball you think you can reach. Go out after it until he calls you off it.

index

Little League Library